d 9⁹⁵
-signed

GARGOYLES & GENTLEMEN

GARGOYLES & GENTLEMEN

A History of St. Paul's Cathedral, London, Ontario

1834-1964

Orlo Miller

Orlo Miller
Apr. 14/973

Toronto
The Ryerson Press

PRINTED AND BOUND IN CANADA
BY THE RYERSON PRESS, TORONTO

This book is respectfully dedicated to
The Right Reverend George Nasmith Luxton, B.A., D.D., LL.D.,
Lord Bishop of Huron
&
The Very Reverend Kenneth Bernard Keefe, D.D.,
Dean of Huron

CONTENTS

ILLUSTRATIONS

PROLOGUE

In one respect at least, time has been kind to the old church.

The community she serves has expanded more than thirty-fold in the one hundred and seventeen years since she was built. The motor omnibus has replaced the stagecoach—and the convertible, the brougham—but the "elegant vista" that enchanted her architect survives to delight the eye of the twentieth-century visitor.

Progress has hemmed her in with brick and steel and mortar but her view of the valley of the Canadian Thames whose waters bore her vice-regal sponsor to the site of the city nearly two centuries ago is still unobstructed by anything but the trees that verge the river and the high board fence around the riverside estate of one of her early supporters, Captain John Harris, R.N. (Ret.).

History came to St. Paul's Cathedral down Fullarton Street, which commemorates the wife of an early parishioner.

Fullarton Street is two blocks long. At one end is the cathedral, at the other the Harris estate. The neat cottages with their white picket fences that once framed the view of the river from St. Paul's have given place to office buildings, industrial establishments and used car lots, but nothing else has changed.

The two blocks of Fullarton Street represent the past. St. Paul's resolutely faces the past with her faded pink-tinted porch, while her high-hipped, red-bricked rear spurns the mushrooming metropolis behind her.

St. Paul's *is* history. Her records take us back to colonial days and her tattered battle flags bring us down the years to Ypres and Dieppe.

To the mind oppressed by the nuclear policy of nations, yesterday is easier to contemplate than tomorrow and St. Paul's *is* yesterday.

To her doors once came the members of the Minor Establishment . . . the merchant princes, the lettered and unlettered colonial squirearchy, the braided martinets, the money-lenders and the factory-owners, the financially-embarrassed sons of peers and the enriched daughters of nobodies, the politically proud and the temporally meek, the shapers of history and the fomenters of rebellion.

Her bells have tolled for knights and condemned criminals . . . for weddings and days of national mourning . . . to signal victory and to herald calamity . . . to praise God and to honour the king.

She is a church . . . a beached ship . . . the Ark of the Covenant . . . a building of weathered brick and wood.

By herself, she is this and nothing more.

It is the lives she has blessed, the loves she has sanctified, the deaths she has glorified, that make her worthy of record.

This is the story of the priests and people of St. Paul's, London, Ontario, cathedral church of the Anglican Diocese of Huron.

CHAPTER ONE

WILDERNESS

What went ye out into the wilderness to see? A reed shaken with the wind? But what went ye out for to see? A man clothed in soft raiment? behold, they that wear soft clothing are in kings' houses.

Matthew 11: 7-8

When the first permanent settlers came to Southwestern Ontario the peninsula was thickly blanketed by a forest of great age—a wilderness of immense trees.

The untouched forest was hated or loved, depending on the psychology of the observer and his reason for being there. The Indians and the French *coureurs-de-bois* saw it in one light; the nature-loving European travellers of the eighteenth and early nineteenth centuries, in another. The white settlers loathed it.

The first two groups, being illiterate, left no record of their feelings about the forest. We can only speculate. The third group has left us a library of rich and ornate prose. One of the most romantic of these is the account written in 1721 by Father Pierre François Xavier de Charlevoix of a journey by canoe along the north shore of Lake Erie. In a much-quoted passage which was later to influence the policy of the first lieutenant-governor of the province, the good father declaims in lyrical prose:

Wherever I went ashore I was quite enchanted by the beauty and variety of a landscape which was terminated by the noblest forests in the whole world. Were we always to sail as I did, with a serene sky in a most charming climate, and on water as clear as the purest fountain, we might possibly be tempted to travel so to the end of our days.

This is almost pure Rousseau. The "noble forests" and the crystal waters are treated as a painted backdrop for a portrait

1

of the "noble savage." Nothing is said of the clouds of black-
flies by day and mosquitoes by night or of the stench of the
Indian villages. Nothing is said of the perpetual twilight that
prevailed in the woods or the effect of these dark and grim
surroundings on the minds of men, civilized and uncivilized
alike.

Accustomed as we are to the tame, second-growth saplings
that timber the woodlots and the remaining waste spaces of
the peninsula today, we are inclined to underestimate the task
that faced the settlers in clearing their land. The term "forest
giant" was no hyperbole. These great trees frequently towered
two hundred feet into the wilderness skies and were packed
as tightly together as sardines in a can. A keen-eyed American
traveller described the pine woods between Ingersoll and
London in 1832 in these words:

A short distance further westward our road leads us into a dense
forest, exclusively of white pine. . . The mind of man can hardly
image a more interesting wilderness scene than is here presented
to the eye of the tourist. . . The regular and elegant wall of trees
on either hand whose spiral tops reach (seemingly) to the heavens,
their beautiful evergreen hue, the deep impervious shade beneath
their small and straight yet intertwining branches, all, viewed together, appears at once pleasing, sublime and solemn. Some of the
trees are very large and in no other place have I seen a forest so
compact, such a vast quantity of timber on any particular space
of ground.

In sum, the Ontario forest as it stood at the beginning of
the nineteenth century was a wonderful subject for descrip-
tive prose but a terrifying and oppressive setting for a home.
In other words it was a fine place to visit, but who would want
to live there?

Apparently quite a few people did. They began coming
in the last decade of the eighteenth century. They came, not
because of the scenic attractions of the province, but because
it offered a refuge from persecution.

The War of the American Revolution which cost Britain
her North American colonies, left several thousand royalist
supporters either homeless, or hounded by their republican
neighbours. Ten thousand of these United Empire Loyalists

poured into the virgin territories west of Montreal after the signing of the peace in 1784.

With them they brought their church—the Church of England.

The first shepherds of the flock were army chaplains and the first churches were small chapels in the various army barracks. In Southwestern Ontario the first chaplain was probably attached to Butler's Rangers and the first chapel was at the Rangers' headquarters in Fort Niagara on the American side of the Niagara River. After the signing of the peace, services were conducted at Butlersbury (now the village of Niagara-on-the-Lake) on the Canadian side.

The first separate Anglican church building to be erected in Ontario still stands—Her Majesty's Chapel of the Mohawks, near Brantford, built in 1787. With the help of their chaplain, the Reverend Dr. John Stuart, the Anglican Mohawks of the Six Nations Confederacy removed from their ancient home in New York State to the Grand River after the close of the war, bringing with them some of the silver communion vessels given them by Queen Anne in 1712. The first communion service to be held in the present Diocese of Huron was celebrated in this church by Dr. Stuart in June, 1784.

The Canada Act, passed by the British Parliament in 1791. set aside the newly-settled region west of Montreal as a new province to be known as Upper Canada. With the passage of the Act, the appointment of Colonel John Graves Simcoe, a veteran of the American Revolutionary War, as the first lieutenant-governor, and the setting aside of certain wild lands for the support of a "Protestant clergy," the work of the Church of England on the frontier was put on a more formal basis.

Prior to the passage of the Act, the Right Reverend Charles Inglis, first bishop of Nova Scotia—whose ecclesiastical jurisdiction included as well the British colonies of Upper and Lower Canada, New Brunswick, Bermuda and Newfoundland—appealed to the Society for the Propagation of the Gospel in Foreign Parts (SPG), for a missionary to serve the Niagara region where there was a numerous settlement of Loyalists.

With the financial assistance of a number of the leading residents of the area—including Colonel John Butler, commander of the disbanded corps bearing his name—a missionary priest was appointed in 1791. He was the Reverend Robert Addison, a graduate of Trinity College, Cambridge.

Addison arrived at Butlersbury, which by then had changed its name to Newark, in the summer of 1792. The village was to be his home and the headquarters for his labours for the next thirty-seven years. Soon after his arrival work was begun on the building of a church at Newark—St. Mark's, today one of the oldest church buildings in the province.

St. Mark's, the Chapel of the Mohawks and the pioneer church at Sandwich presided over by the Reverend Richard Pollard, former sheriff of Detroit, were the first three Anglican churches of the western peninsula. Before the eighteenth century was out a fourth church was being built at the village of Delaware, in Middlesex County.

Ebenezer Allen, founder of Rochester, New York, as well as of Delaware village, was the church's builder. Nothing in his previous career prepares us for the picture of Allen as a dedicated churchman. Born in New Jersey, he lived a relatively uneventful and colourless life as a miller until the approach of his fortieth birthday when the American colonies revolted against the rule of Britain. From that time on until his death in 1816 Allen endured enough excitement to satisfy three normal men.

A close acquaintance with the ways of the Indians, gained during the French-Indian wars of the mid-eighteenth century, led him into service as a scout attached to the Loyalist forces at Fort Niagara. Colonel John Butler of Butler's Rangers and Colonel John Johnson of the Indian Department employed him on many delicate missions. From this work and his polygamous habits among the aborigines he gained the nickname "Indian" Allen.

Allen took on many of the characteristics of his Indian friends, including a sometimes shaky loyalty to the British cause. Not to put too fine a point on it, he turned his coat on occasion and worked for and with the rebels. As a result of one such final escapade he ended his war service as a prisoner in the military jail at Montreal.

After the signing of the peace in 1784 he returned to the American side and built a mill on the Genesee River which became the nucleus of Rochester. Subsequently, learning of the free lands available in Upper Canada, he reminded the new lieutenant-governor, Colonel John Graves Simcoe, of his services to the Crown and asked for a grant of two thousand acres in what is now the county of Middlesex.

Simcoe was at this time on a tour of the western country during which he visited the present site of the City of London. He was much taken by the military advantages of the site— at the forks of a partially-navigable stream, some distance from the American border—and determined that he would locate here the capital of the new province. He renamed the river, previously called by the Indians, Askunesippi (Antlered River), and by the French, La Tranche, as the Thames. His proposed capital he called London. His plan was vetoed by the Home Office in England but the names "London" and "Thames" continued to be applied in the region. When the province was divided into administrative districts in 1800 one was named the District of London. It was a very large tract, extending from Lake Erie to Lake Huron and from the town of Simcoe on the east almost to Chatham on the west. When the townships within the district were surveyed, that immediately to the north of the forks of the Thames River was also named after Simcoe's projected capital.

In spite of "Indian" Allen's chequered career his request for land was viewed favourably by Simcoe and he was granted a large block of land in Delaware Township, west of London, on certain conditions. He was to erect on the site, within a reasonable time, a mill and a church to serve as the nucleus for a settlement. The church, of course, was intended for use by the Church of England.

The mill was apparently completed, but nothing more than the frame of the church was ever erected. It seems that Allen ran out of money before he could finish the job. Being in this case, as ever a resourceful man, he endeavoured to repair the deficiency by coining the required number of Spanish "pieces of eight" in the basement of the mill. His counterfeits of the eight real piece, often called a "Mexican dollar" (legalized currency of the Province of Upper Canada under one of the first acts of the provincial legislature) were obviously artistically inadequate, for the unfeeling authorities arrested him and salted him away in the district dungeon in the Long Point area for an undetermined period.

The skeleton of the first Anglican church in Middlesex County mouldered away without ever having witnessed a service. Its builder's later career fulfilled earlier expectations. Allen saw the inside of the London District Gaol on at least one other occasion, the charge being theft of an axe. No one ever saw fit to charge him with the obvious offence of bigamy. in spite of the fact that at one time his *ménage* at Delaware included four wives, two white and two Indian.

In the light of his previous war record Allen came under the suspicion of the military authorities during the War of 1812-1814. A one-time neighbour, close friend and fellow Indian scout, Andrew Westbrooke, deserted to the American forces early in the war and organized a band of brigands who periodically ravaged the settlements in the interior of the peninsula. Allen was suspected of giving aid and comfort to his old friend, but the charge seems to have been unsubstantiated. The greying old rogue died on his farm at Delaware in 1816, paterfamilias to a large assortment of genetically-varied offspring one at least of whom achieved a posthumous notoriety almost the equal of his parent by being tortured to death by Sioux Indians during the California gold rush.

The ravages of the war with the United States together with the effects of a widespread crop failure in 1816—"the year without a summer"—left the western settlements decimated and badly shaken. By 1818 however the townships were beginning to fill up with a tide of United Kingdom immigrants, forced from their homes by the acute financial depression of the post-Napoleonic period.

Among the immigrants were both "church" and "chapel" folk, with perhaps a preponderance of the former. Some of the earliest members of the congregation of St. Paul's Cathedral were among these arrivals, among them the Carling and Cornish families.

Among the first to arrive was Richard S. Talbot, an Anglican country squire from Tipperary County, Ireland, who
brought with him a complete settlement of Tipperary Protes-
tants. An account of their arrival appeared in *The Gleaner*,
an early newspaper published in the town of Niagara, in its
issue of September 17th, 1818:

Arrived on Sunday morning on board the schooner *Caledonia*,
fifty settlers from the County of Tipperary, Ireland, accompanied
by a gentleman from that place of the name of Richard Talbot,
who, by an arrangement made with Lord Bathurst by advancing
ten pounds with each adult had their passage across the Atlantic
provided for them and five weeks' provision with a promise of
one hundred acres of land to each male above seventeen years of
age. The money advanced to be refunded as soon as they are
settled upon their lands. One hundred and sixty came out with
Mr. Talbot under that arrangement, *viz.* sixty males and one
hundred females.

The Talbot settlers established themselves in London
Township, a few miles north of the present city. The names
of these settlers, their leader and his talented sons appear
many times in the records of the Anglican Church in the
London area.

It is probable that some of these sturdy Irishmen met the
Honourable and Reverend Charles James Stewart, first formal
missionary of the SPG on his visit to the western area in 1820.
Certainly most of the colony met him on his second tour two
years later, described in the next chapter.

Stewart, a son of the Earl of Galloway, entered the Canadian missionary field in 1807, working first for several years
in the Eastern Townships of Quebec. After the war of 1812
he returned to England to obtain financial and moral support
for extended Canadian missions. Having received it, he
mapped out an extensive tour of the western part of the
province.

Because of his dedicated work in Lower Canada Stewart
has been called the "Apostle of the Eastern Townships."
He deserves a similar acknowledgment for his work in western
Upper Canada. He may with justice be called the "father"
of the Anglican Church in the London area. His missionary
visits of 1820 and 1822 led directly to the establishment of the
congregation of St. Paul's, London.

CHAPTER TWO

MISSION

When he (Jesus) saw the multitudes, he was moved with compassion on them, because they fainted and were scattered abroad, as sheep having no shepherd. Then saith he unto his disciples, The harvest truly is plenteous, but the labourers are few; pray ye therefore the Lord of the harvest, that he will send forth labourers into his harvest.

Matthew 9: 36-38

St. Paul's congregation came into being as a direct result of the second missionary journey to the western portion of the Province of Upper Canada by the Honourable and Reverend Dr. Charles James Stewart.

On this visit, in the summer of 1822, Dr. Stewart preached in a barn in London Township to a surprisingly large congregation of 250 persons. He baptized their children, performed a number of marriages and promised he would try to get them a clergyman.

In a report subsequently made to the Society for the Propagation of the Gospel in Foreign Parts, however, he merely stated that in the townships of Oxford, Westminster and London, the numbers of settlers was rapidly increasing and, "notwithstanding the variety of sects into which the people are divided, it is reasonable to hope that in a short time they will have become sensible of the advantages which arise from an ecclesiastical establishment and, availing themselves of the offers of the Society, will unite their efforts in the building of churches."

Despite the non-committal nature of his report Dr. Stewart eventually kept his promise to the London Township settlers. By the time he did so, however, he had become bishop of the vast Diocese of Quebec and a new, raw little town at the forks of the Canadian Thames River had usurped the priority of the earlier settlement to the north of it.

Dr. Stewart was consecrated Bishop of Quebec on January

21, 1826. In that same month the Legislature of Upper Canada decided to relocate the judicial offices of the huge administrative District of London. The District, named for Lieutenant-Governor Simcoe's dream capital of Upper Canada, took in the territory of some seven modern Western Ontario counties.

Courts for this enormous region had previously been held in the little village of Vittoria, in Norfolk County. When the courts were first established there, Vittoria was the centre of the most extensive settlement in the District. By 1826 however the western townships were rapidly filling up, as Dr. Stewart had indicated, and numerous complaints were being registered by the residents of Middlesex County at the excessive distances they were obliged to travel to transact legal business.

It was decided therefore to relocate the capital in a more central area. The tiny villages of St. Thomas and Delaware set up a noisy clamour for the honour, overdoing it to the extent that the legislators chose neither but selected a compromise site, declaring it "expedient to establish the district town at the reservation heretofore made for a town near the forks of the River Thames, in the townships of Westminster and London."

It was in this manner that Simcoe's dream city of London, Canada finally achieved reality—not, it is true, as the capital of the province but at least as the capital of a district. Political expediency was combined with sentimentality in the choice of the site, for the prime mover in the selection was Lieutenant-Colonel Thomas Talbot who had been Simcoe's aide-de-camp on his visit to the area in 1793.

Certainly the site was chosen without regard to the nature of the terrain. London had been settled for nearly fifty years before the last of the bogs, marshes, stream beds and quicksand deposits were filled in, covered over or drained. Many of them still lie in wait for unsuspecting contractors.

The survey of the site was completed in the late summer of 1826 and the first building—a log shanty doubling as a house and inn—was erected by one of the chain-bearers on the survey party, Peter MacGregor, on October 1.

Almost immediately thereafter construction began of a two-storey frame building to serve as a temporary courthouse and jail. It was used for the first time at the sitting of the Court of Assizes in January, 1827.

The first building to be built in London was a tavern, and the second, a jail—a reasonably logical sequence of events. There was no Anglican church for some time and there exists no record of regular church services of any denomination for the first two years. Time not spent by the handful of inhabitants in the pursuit of their daily labours seems to have been expended in libations and litigation. The picture commonly presented of the earliest pioneers of Ontario as God-fearing, trusting and trustworthy subjects of the King is not borne out by the court records.

In London, as in most of the smaller and newer towns and villages throughout the province, the Methodist circuit riders were the first to bring the Gospel to the people. They lived off the land and were not bound by the cumbersome ecclesiastical machinery of the more orthodox—and established—churches.

Occasionally the Methodists ran foul of the law which had established the Church of England as the state church of Upper Canada. Under the establishment, marriages could be performed only by an Anglican priest (by publication of banns or licence) or by an authorized justice of the peace (by licence only).

Shortly after the close of the War of 1812 one Henry Ryan, a Methodist circuit rider, performed an illegal marriage ceremony in Westminster Township, south of London. He was charged with the offence, arrested, tried and found guilty. His sentence was barbarous—transportation for fourteen years to the penal colony of Van Diemen's Land (Tasmania). The indignation of the Methodists of Upper Canada was intense and its effects were almost immediately felt by the provincial authorities. The sentence was suspended and Ryan went free, but the incident played its part in the eventual disestablishment of the Church of England.

The case of Henry Ryan shows the continuing efforts of the evangelical churches to obtain footholds in the back-country areas. Although no reliable records are available, it is more than likely that some form of Methodist services, albeit on a sporadic basis, were available to the citizens of the infant community of London almost from the beginning.

There are fleeing glimpses of missionary visits by Roman Catholic priests to the settlement in its first two years and an occasional notation of baptisms and marriages performed by the Reverend Alexander Macintosh, Anglican priest at the mission in St. Thomas, eighteen miles south of London, which was opened in 1824. Since Macintosh, in addition to his regular charge in St. Thomas, was responsible also for five other stations in as many different townships, his statement respecting London village that "the service is performed almost too seldom to be denominated occasional" was only too true.

On August 2, 1828, Bishop Stewart again visited the area and held a service in the temporary courthouse. On that occasion representations were made to him of the need for a missionary in the village. It took the bishop just over a year to find the funds and the man to establish a mission in London.

The funds were supplied by the Society for the Propagation of the Gospel. The man was the Reverend Edward Jukes Boswell.

Boswell was born in England in 1798. He was ordained deacon in 1827, but whether in England or Canada cannot now be determined, and posted to St. John's Sandwich on the Detroit River frontier. He was transferred from that parish with orders to set up the London mission in August, 1829. He was priested by Bishop Stewart the following year.

The exact date of Boswell's arrival in London is not known but he performed seven baptisms in the village on August 23, 1829. These are the first entries in the earliest register of St. Paul's Cathedral, a fine ragpaper ledger carrying an 1825 watermark.

The names of the parents and sponsors in the first group of records form direct links with the earliest settlements in the western portion of the province. Benjamin Schram and John Freleigh were sons of members of Colonel John Butler's Corps of Rangers. Their fathers had attended services conducted by the Reverend John Addison at Fort Niagara and later at Butlersbury. Catherine Dingman was the daughter of a Ranger. Francis Lewis, Alexander Guffin, Rebecca Ardell, Maria Sifton, Margaret Shoebottom and Anne Talbot were members of the Irish Anglican settlement established a few miles north of London by Richard Talbot of Tipperary in 1818. Most of them had probably attended the service conducted in Geary's barn by Dr. Stewart in 1822.

One or two of the names in these first entries have a distinctly un-Anglican sound. Hugh McCandless and Felix McLaughlin were probably not members of the Church of England but when it came to the important business of baptizing one's child into the Kingdom of God, an Anglican padre in hand was better than two Roman Catholic priests in the bush. Ecumenicity was not a doctrine of the early settlers so much as it was a necessity.

The names imposed upon the helpless babes were typical of the times—Mary Catherine, John, Deborah, Elizabeth, Sally, Adam and Rosina. With the exception of the last-named they were all good, staunch, roastbeef-and-Yorkshire-pudding kinds of names.

During the three years he was stationed in London, Edward Boswell baptized 159 children and adults. Most of the Sarahs and Betties and Ralphs and Williams and Isaacs and Johns and Henrys are lost to history, their memories preserved only in half-forgotten family records or half-obliterated memorial stones. However four of those who were marked with the sign of Christ are still remembered for achievements in politics and on the stage and for notoriety in the gentle art of dying.

The first of the quartet was John, son of Thomas and Margaret Carling, born January 23, 1828, in the Township of London and baptized by E. J. Boswell in the village of London on April 11, 1830.

John Carling together with his brother Isaac (three years his senior but baptized on the same day) later founded the Carling Breweries. John entered politics in the 1850's, first as a member of London's municipal council and later as a federal member of Parliament. He played an active part in both the pre- and post-Confederation national planning, became a federal minister of agriculture and was knighted by Queen Victoria in 1893. From the first establishment of the congregation of St. Paul's to the present the Carling family has played an active and honourable role in the work of the Anglican Church of Canada.

So much cannot be said for the second member of the quartet, although it cannot be denied that he made his mark.

Francis Evans Cornish, the son of William King Cornish and Elizabeth Catherine his wife was born also in London township, on February 1, 1831, and was baptized by E. J. Boswell on the 27th of the same month.

Cornish followed his father into the profession of the law and in the mid-1850's became one of the youngest Queen's Counsellors ever to be named in Canada. Soon thereafter he entered municipal politics and after serving a couple of terms as alderman, was elected mayor in 1861. He retained the post for four years by the exercise of techniques that put the worst days of Tammany Hall to shame. He was only ousted from the mayoralty when his fellow-councillors called out the militia to ensure an honest election.

Cornish's public and private career was high-lighted by charges of bigamy, assault and drunkenness and by noisy, public disputes with the Commander-in-Chief of the British armed forces in Canada, the London chief of police and other assorted local and national dignitaries. He was a legendary figure during and after his lifetime and ended his days as first mayor of the city of Winnipeg and first member of the federated Parliament for the riding of Poplar Point, a campaign which he won by the simple expedient of kidnapping his opponent on the eve of the election.

So much for now. The shadow of Francis Evans Cornish will fall frequently on these pages.

Graves Simcoe Lee, the third of the four famous persons baptized by E. J. Boswell, was born in the village of London on December 1, 1828, and baptized on September 28, 1831. He was the son of Dr. Hiram Davis Lee and his wife Anne (Terry) Lee both of whom were children of United Empire

Loyalists. Their son, Graves Simcoe, was named in honour of the first Lieutenant-Governor of the Province.

The Lees had been physicians for generations, first in England and later in Connecticut and in Upper Canada. Graves Simcoe was destined for the same profession. However in early youth he became fascinated by the amateur theatricals staged by the officers of the British garrison, then stationed in London, and took part in some of their plays.

From the moment he first appeared on the stage he was lost to medicine and eventually made his way to the professional American stage where he became one of the brighter lights of Broadway and the touring companies in the 1860's. He was the first of an illustrious line of theatrical celebrities, both amateur and professional, who claimed London as their home town and St. Paul's as their home parish.

The fourth VIP to be baptized by young Mr. Boswell was notorious rather than famous. His head became known to more persons through the civilized world than that of any other single, *named* person in history. (So far as is known, the owners of the original Neanderthal skull and the Piltdown forgery were never christened.) However, he was never in a position adequately to appreciate his fame, which came to him posthumously.

Properly to tell the story of Cornelius Alverson Burleigh it is necessary to recreate as nearly as possible conditions in the village of London as they existed in the summer of 1830. It may be that this is the best way of telling the story of the earliest days of the mission which became St. Paul's parish.

Besides it will increase the suspense.

Between his arrival in late August and the end of the year 1829, Boswell was kept busy organizing his congregation and performing marriages (fourteen) and baptisms (sixteen). Services were held in the homes of leading Anglicans, there being no church or building set aside for that purpose.

The missionary attempted to rectify this situation by appearing before the justices of the peace "in general quarter sessions assembled" in January, 1830, to ask permission to use a room in the nearly-completed new courthouse for the purpose of Sunday services.

On January 16 he received a letter from Colonel Mahlon Burwell, chairman of the sessions, and a staunch Anglican:

The receipt of your favour respecting the want of a house in which to perform Divine service and requesting permission to use the Court-Room is acknowledged. The magistrates instruct me to inform you that, as the Court-House is the property of the District, erected for the only purpose of accommodating His Majesty's Courts of Law in the administration of justice, they do not conceive that they possess the right of granting you your request.

Parenthetically it may be commented that many of Colonel Burwell's fellow magistrates were Methodists.

The courthouse here referred to was not the frame building constructed in 1827, but a handsome new permanent structure modeled along the lines of Malahide Castle near Dublin, Ireland, ancestral home of Lieutenant-Colonel Thomas Talbot. Most early travellers, unaware of the delicate compliment being paid to the redoubtable Colonel, referred to it in rather slighting terms as being "somewhat Gothic." It was also somewhat expensive for the time and the place, having cost more than £4,000 (provincial currency, equal to $16,000 American).

Boswell subsequently received permission to hold Sunday services in the "schoolhouse" on the main square. This was the old temporary courthouse. From its erection in 1827 until the completion of the permanent building it had served a triple purpose as courthouse, jail and school. The rear half of the first floor reinforced with logs, palisade-fashion, was the jail, the front half contained the courtroom and school was kept in the loft. After the cells and legal offices were removed, the whole building was turned over to the use of the "grammar school" authorities. A "grammar school" was an early nineteenth-century version of a modern secondary school. The curriculum was heavy on the classics and attendance was pretty well limited to the "better" families.

This hastily built but well-constructed frame building was home for the congregation of St. Paul's for a total of nearly five years. It stood without major alteration for a century until torn down to make way for the London city police station in the mid-1920's.

While the courtroom in the new building was already in use by January, 1830, prisoners were still being lodged in the temporary structure. The most celebrated prisoner of the year was Cornelius Burleigh.

"Con" Burleigh had been charged with a petty theft in the fall of 1829 and a warrant issued for his arrest. A district constable, Timothy Conklin Pomeroy, was assigned to execute the warrant. He tracked Burleigh to his home neighbourhood in Bayham Township on Lake Erie. Burleigh, being warned of the constable's approach, hid out in the bush.

"Con," a farm labourer whose mentality approached sub-moronic level, was terrified at the prospect of arrest. At least one man had actually been hanged in the District for theft under the brutal and as yet unreformed English criminal code. "Con" feared the worst and in his extremity turned to some friends, three male members of a family named Ribble. The Ribbles sheltered him for some time until Constable Pomeroy smelled them out.

One dark night on a lonely forest road Tim Pomeroy walked into an ambush. A shot was fired and Tim died. An investigation was immediately launched. Search of the murder site revealed a single clue—an abandoned cap, subsequently identified as the property of "Con" Burleigh.

Burleigh and the three Ribbles were arrested and lodged in the primitive jail at London to await trial at the spring assizes.

The case was duly reported in London's two newspapers. So rapidly had the village grown in importance in its less than four years of existence that two enterprising residents had seen fit to risk their capital in the effort to meet its need for communication media. As one of the two proprietors stated in his flowery prospectus:

Enjoying all the blessings of our unparalleled constitution . . . we need only the aid of that powerful engine the press, to spread throughout the world a knowledge of our situation and invite from every nation, the industrious and enterprising.

Feeling this to be our situation and anxious to see the whole wilderness converted into smiling fields and the abode of the wolf and the haunt of the savage become the asylums of the sons and daughters of liberty and civilization, we have determined, by the establishment of a Press in London, to contribute our mite towards the attainment of those ends.

The author of this magnificent specimen of hyperbole was an Anglican and a member of Reverend Mr. Boswell's congregation. He was Edward Allen Talbot, son of the Richard Talbot whose group of Irish emigrants inaugurated the first large-scale settlement in London Township in 1818. The young Talbot was not only London's first newspaper editor, but the author at twenty years of age of one of the most-widely circulated books on settlement in Upper Canada— *Five Years' Residence in the Canadas,* published in England in 1824.

Talbot's paper, *The London Sun,* was a secular weekly. The rival journal was ostensibly a religious paper called *The Wesleyan Advocate,* a semi-official organ of the Wesleyan Methodist Church. Its editor was, in his way, every bit as colourful as the editor of *The Sun.* He was The Reverend James Jackson, a native of the United States and a cousin of General Andrew Jackson ("Old Hickory") victor of the Battle of New Orleans (1815) who became the seventh president of the United States. London, incidentally, was well supplied with kin of famous Americans at this period. John and Oliver McClary, London residents who later founded the McClary Manufacturing Company (now General Steel Wares) were cousins of John Adams, second president of the United States and John Quincy Adams, sixth president.

Before the spring assizes were held both newspapers had occasion to print a sensational story. There had been a whole-sale break of prisoners from the makeshift jail. All the prisoners but one had made good their escape. So assured of his innocence was "Con" Burleigh that he elected to remain behind. Since he was charged jointly with the three Ribbles on the murder indictment, his trial was laid over to the summer assizes.

Burleigh's three co-defendants enjoyed their liberty for a brief time only. By the time the officials assembled in the partly-completed new courthouse on a sweltering August day, all four were safely ensconced in their cells. Meanwhile Edward Boswell and his congregation had not been idle. Land had been secured early in the year from the Government, at the northwest corner of Ridout and Dundas streets and on this the frame of a church building had been erected by the congregation. The lot was substantial—two and a half acres—and so was the church, the frame being eighty feet long by forty in width. Beside the frame of the church was the graveyard and at least one fresh grave—that of Lawrence Lawrason who died on March 9 at the age of seventy years. Lawrason was a veteran of the American Revolutionary War, a United Empire Loyalist and founder of one of London's oldest families. The tombstone erected by the survivors can be seen today in the cathedral grounds.

The assizes offered the only entertainment available at this period to the people of the district and soon accommodation in the village hotels was at a premium. Although the criminal docket was a heavy one, interest centred from the beginning on the Pomeroy murder case—perhaps because it involved the violent death of a peace officer or more likely because of the circumstantial nature of the Crown's case.

The Reverend James Jackson took a personal interest in the defence of the three members of the Ribble family. They were land-owners and, possibly, Methodists. The reasoning of Jackson and other defenders of the Ribbles seems to have been that a verdict against them would cost the lives of three church-going taxpayers while an unfavourable decision by the jurors against Burleigh would result in no hardship to anyone except, of course, Burleigh himself.

The Ribbles were tried first. Before court assembled that August morning everyone in town including the potential jurymen had in his hands a printed document purporting to be the confession of Cornelius Alverson Burleigh to the murder of Timothy Conklin Pomeroy. It was a very literate affair which blamed the whole unhappy matter upon Burleigh's sinful predilection for the joys of the dance. This, plus the fact that the production came from the press of *The Wesleyan Advocate*, points unmistakably to the Reverend James Jackson as the instigator of the project and the author of the "confession" and its precise timing.

The issue was inevitable. The Ribbles were acquitted and "Con" Burleigh was sentenced to be hanged. The execution took place three days later in front of the courthouse. "Con" was hanged in the presence of three thousand witnesses. (The total population of the village at this time was less than three hundred.)

The spectators at this Roman holiday got more than their money's worth. It turned out to be a "double feature." The parsimonious officials had provided an unsound rope which snapped as Burleigh went through the trap. While the half-choked victim staggered about among the crowd, exhorting them incoherently to repentance, someone nipped across the street to the general store operated by George Jervis Goodhue, a Connecticut Yankee who was a member of the Reverend Mr. Boswell's congregation, and purchased a new rope. "Con" went through the trap again while blue-smocked yeomen held up their children to witness the condemned man's last, grisly dance.

Although the Burleigh "confession" intimated that Jackson was the spiritual advisor for the condemned man, it was the Reverend Edward J. Boswell who attended him at the scaffold and who also baptized him in the rites of the Church of England prior to his execution. The record, in the first register of St. Paul's Church, reads:

Cornelius A Burley [sic] *a condemned criminal—aged as he supposed about 26 or 27—Baptized 19th Augt. 1830.*

The double hanging of Cornelius Burleigh did not end the day's entertainment. In accordance with custom the body was turned over to the local medical men. The only cadavers available to practising physicians and their students were those of paupers without relatives and executed criminals. The ensuing dissection of Burleigh's corpse was, like the execution, a public spectacle.

Nor was even this the end of the humiliation to which poor, stupid Con's earthly clay was subjected.

By chance there was a young student from Yale University in London that day. The young man's name was then unknown to fame; a later generation would know it as a household word. He was Orson Squires Fowler, who made the pseudo-science of phrenology the base of one of the largest personal fortunes in nineteenth-century North America.

Fowler begged Burleigh's head of the medical fraternity. Receiving his boon, he lugged the grisly trophy off, stripped the skull of flesh and cured it. Later—some reports say the same night—he used the skull to demonstrate the various bumps and hollows which, according to him, illustrated the facets of unhappy Con's character.

Fowler took the skull with him when he left London. Throughout his long public career it accompanied him wherever he went. In his thousands of public appearances before the rich and poor, the common people and the "crowned heads of Europe" Burleigh's skull was his demonstration piece, his "gimmick." The top of the skull had been neatly sawed off, so that a candle could be inserted. When the top was fitted on again, the light showed the varying thicknesses of the skull upon which Fowler's art or "science" depended.

After having been viewed by more persons than the skull of any other baptized person in history, the head was returned to London during Fowler's last North American tour and deposited through some chance with the Harris family of Eldon House. The skull, minus the important sawn-off top, may be seen today at Eldon House, now an historic site operated by the London Public Library.

By an interesting coincidence, the Harris property was purchased in October, 1832, by John Harris from the Reverend Edward J. Boswell, who had baptized Cornelius Burleigh.

That then is the story of the fourth member of the quartet of celebrated persons whom Edward Boswell baptized during the three years and two months that he served the mission of London.

As the missionary ended his first full year of service he had cause to be pleased with the accomplishments of himself and his congregation. He himself had been ordered priest at Montreal in July. He had secured land for a church and the congregation had begun the erection of a house of worship on it. His year-end report to the SPG was optimistic:

I have only a school house in which to perform Divine Service but I trust that as the frame of a church has been erected this summer the inhabitants may be able to finish it next year.

CHAPTER THREE

PLAGUE

And while the flesh was yet between their teeth, ere it was chewed, the wrath of the Lord was kindled against the people, and the Lord smote the people with a very great plague.

Numbers 11: 33

Boswell's optimism in his church and congregation was in the result unjustified. For reasons now unknown the huge frame of the uncompleted church at the corner of Dundas and Ridout streets remained unfinished and untenanted throughout the missionary's stay in London.

Compared with the previous year, 1831 was a "quiet time." Little of interest occurred in the village or within the congregation. At the rectory the only incident to break the even succession of entries of births, marriages and deaths in the parish register was the priests' occasionally running out of ink. Thus, for example, in the church register under date of November 1, 1831 under the record of the marriage of William Dann and Sarah Rawlins, we see this notation by Boswell:

No Ink in the house. Could not get the signatures of the parties —took notes of registry at the house.

This ink shortage occurred two or three times, always at the first of the month. We are left to speculate whether this recurring situation was due to a supply problem in the remote frontier hamlet or whether the missionary's own meagre stipend gave out at each month's end.

Our curiosity must also remain unsatisfied about Boswell's place of residence. As mentioned in the last chapter, Boswell owned the property on which the Harris family later built their home, Eldon House, having purchased it from John

Kent sometime in 1831. Whether the "house" Boswell refers to in the above notation was on this property or not, is not known.

The schoolhouse continued to be the site of Sunday services. For some reason Boswell re-applied for its use to the bench of magistrates on April 15, 1831, and permission was granted.

At the beginning of the new year, 1832, Boswell apparently decided to push ahead with the matter of the uncompleted church. An article from *The London Sun,* reprinted in *The Courier of Upper Canada,* reported in March that "at the suggestion of the members (of the congregation), the Rev. Mr. Boswell was induced to apply to the lieutenant-governor in council for permission to sell about one-half acre of the reserve, it being utterly unfit for a graveyard."

The newspaper account adds that permission had been granted and eight building lots, each thirty by eighty feet, would be auctioned shortly at an anticipated price of £75 to £125 each.

From another source we learn that Boswell's proposal had been endorsed by Lieutenant-Colonel Thomas Talbot, doughty patriarch of the Talbot settlement. In a letter to the land committee of the executive council of Upper Canada dated February 20, 1832, the Colonel wrote:

Two half-acre lots were reserved in the village plot of London for a Protestant church and churchyard. Viz.: No. 21 for the church and No. 22 for the churchyard, both on the north side of Dundas Street. There has been a substantial frame erected for the church but which is not covered in and consequently is daily receiving injury from the weather. Mr. Boswell is of opinion that such of the ground as the church does not occupy could be sold for a sufficient sum to finish the church, which certainly would be desirable.

Once again the Anglicans of London seem to have been somewhat unfairly dealt with by the authorities. As *The Sun* stated, an apparently favourable answer had been received from the land committee, but on April 17 the decision was reversed and Boswell was told the government opposed the sale of the land and would agree only to authorize an exchange for better land.

No such exchange was made and services continued to be held in the schoolhouse. While these quarters were probably adequate in the summer months, the building was miserably cold in the winter. A Presbyterian minister who later preached there noted in his diary:

I preached in the morning to about thirty persons from Matthew 4: 1-12. The depth of the snow was the reason, I suppose, why there were so few persons present. The schoolhouse is very cold and I shall not willingly preach in it again in winter.

The "quiet time" was over. With the coming of the spring of 1832 the village of London and the British colony in which it served as an insignificant regional capital entered upon a severe period of testing.

The sailing vessels began leaving the ports of the United Kingdom as soon as the ice broke up on the St. Lawrence River. Each bore its full, and often overfull, quota of emigrants bound for the free lands of Upper Canada. By early summer the tide was at full flow. There were tens of thousands of them. Immigration records show that no less than ninety-two thousand arrived in Canada that year, most of them from the British Isles.

The ships were rickety, overcrowded and underprovisioned. The immigrants were packed into their holds like cattle. Most of the vessels were little more than floating pigsties. Privacy was nonexistent.

Under these conditions, on voyages lasting from four to eight weeks, the spread of contagious disease was inevitable. Unfortunately the upsurge in immigration coincided with a particularly violent outbreak of Asiatic cholera in the United Kingdom.

The epidemic originated in India in 1827 and in the ensuing years slowly made its way through Asia Minor and thence into Europe. The disease made a successful lodgement in the crowded and filthy slums of the larger English cities and spread wtih appalling speed and virulence. The mortality rate seems to have been higher in Europe and North America than in the homeland of the disease probably because the people of the western lands had built up no resistance to its ravages.

Few immigrant vessels arrived in Canada with a full quota of passengers. Death and burial of cholera victims on the high seas were an almost daily occurrence aboard the ships. On arrival in Canada precautions were taken to prevent the spread of the disease, with some success at first. Grosse Isle— the "Island of Death"—in the St. Lawrence River, was the first stop for all vessels. Here overworked immigration officials endeavoured to check the incidence of disease and to hold vessels in quarantine until a clear bill of health could be given.

What happened was of course inevitable. A passenger carrying the disease escaped official surveillance and got into Quebec City. Within a week the epidemic was raging there and shortly spread to Montreal and thence westward into Upper Canada. By June 10 there were fifty-five cases at Quebec of whom forty-five died within a matter of hours.

The lieutenant-governor of Upper Canada, Sir John Colborne, took immediate action without waiting for the sanction of the legislature. Physicians were appointed to attend the victims and various buildings selected or built for the reception of sufferers. In the District of London hospitals or "pest houses" were opened at Turkey Point, Port Burwell, Port Stanley, on the Longwoods Road in the Township of Cardoc, and in the Village of London.

In London a private residence, built sometime in the mid-1820's on the Hamilton Road by Fells Hubbard, was converted to use as a hospital. The building, some distance from the village limits, was owned in 1832 by Tillery Hubbard, a son of the builder, who had allowed it to fall into disrepair. The building was hastily refitted in two days, barely in time to receive the first victims of the epidemic.

There is no record of the names of the poor immigrants treated here or of the place of burial of those who died. We know only that there were several deaths. None but the utterly destitute went there; district residents who caught the disease were treated in private homes. Many of the latter also died.

The two or three local physicians—including Dr. Hiram Davis Lee, operator of one of the local hotels—were quickly overwhelmed by the volume of cases. In response to their plea for help the government authorities at York sent Dr. John Patrick Donnelly, a former surgeon in the Royal Navy. Donnelly arrived in London on June 30. Exactly one month later he was buried in the graveyard beside the unfinished frame of St. Paul's Church—a victim of the disease he had fought so valiantly to check. Donnelly was a Roman Catholic, and a sad story is told about the unsuccessful search by his unnamed Negro attendant to find a priest to minister to the dying man.

On receipt of the news of Dr. Donnelly's fatal illness the government despatched another Irish physician, Dr. George Moore, to the village. Moore continued to attend the cholera patients assisted by Dr. Elam Stimson until October 5, by which time the danger was past. Moore seems to have escaped the consequences of the disease but Stimson lost his young wife and son, both of whom were buried near Dr. Donnelly.

In the absence of complete records it is difficult to assess the effect of the epidemic on the village. The most accurate account available is that pieced together by the late Dr. Edwin Seaborn in *The March of Medicine in Western Ontario.** From this and from other materials subsequently located, it would appear that the number of deaths resulting from the disease in the village was not less than fifteen and may have been two or three times this figure.

The effect of this number of deaths in a population of little more than three hundred can only be imagined. By mid-August many of the residents had fled the stricken town, taking refuge in the more healthy countryside. By the end of the month the village was practically deserted except for the victims of the plague, the hard-working doctors, the male nurses, the gravediggers—and the Reverend Edward Boswell.

---

*Published by The Ryerson Press: 1944.

Boswell himself left no record of his participation in the events of the epidemic and no trace of his activities can be found in the parish register. He must have baptized some sufferers and buried others, but it was not a time for the keeping of meticulous records.

From the reminiscences of early settlers, set down years later, one heroic story emerges concerning the missionary. It is said that during the height of the epidemic, when the disease was carrying off victims daily, Boswell stationed himself at Blackfriars Bridge on Ridout Street, the main entrance to the village from the north, warning travellers against entering London. How long he maintained his vigil there we do not know.

By September, the cholera had abated sufficiently to permit the holding of the fall assizes in the new courthouse, and the prospects of another public hanging were proving enough to overcome the fear of the plague.

Thousands of district residents plucked up enough courage to go to London for the official taking-off of Henry Sovereign. Sovereign, a farmer of Norfolk County, had once before escaped the gallows. In 1828 he had been sentenced to death for horse-stealing, but the sentence had been remitted. However, while Canadian justice was becoming averse to the exercise of the death penalty in cases of larceny, it still took a decidedly dim view of homicide, particularly when committed on a wholesale scale. The crime for which Sovereign was ceremonially dispatched involved the brutal murder of his wife and six children.

Unlike the case of Burleigh two years before, no sympathy whatever was displayed for the second victim of London's gallows. There seems to have been no doubt of Sovereign's guilt and the trial did not take up much of the court's time. There is no record of the disposal of the condemned man's body. He was apparently attended at the scaffold not by Boswell but by the Reverend Alexander Macintosh, missionary at St. Thomas.

By the first of October life in the village had been restored to normal. On the tenth of the month Boswell officiated at a baptism and a wedding — his last official acts in London.

Shortly thereafter he left the village for a new post in Montreal. The deed of bargain and sale of his property on Ridout Street to John Harris bears the date of October 13. The instrument, as required by law, conveys the property as from the Reverend E. J. Boswell "et ux." This curt legal reference is the only record of any kind referring to Mrs. Boswell, with the exception of a notation in the parish register where *Eliza* Boswell is given as a witness at the marriage of David Knight and Lavina Cowperthwaite on April 5, 1832.

The records of the Anglican Church of Canada give us a few sparse notes about the subsequent career of Edward Jukes Boswell. He later served in parishes at Carleton Place and Williamsburg. On the formation of the Diocese of Ontario he was appointed rector at Prescott, which charge he held until he retired in 1868. He died in Kingston, Ontario on August 26, 1879—almost exactly fifty years after his arrival in London.

No streets, no monuments, no plaques or memorials mark the service given to the congregation of St. Paul's and the community of London by Edward Boswell. Nor are there any memorials to the victims of London's great plague or those who laboured in their behalf. The "five fresh graves" in the cemetery at the foot of Dundas Street to which one writer refers were soon forgotten and the names of those interred there lost to record.

One structure survives to connect the London of today with the terrifying epidemic of 1832. The cholera hospital on the Hamilton Road although somewhat altered in the course of the years and recently damaged inside by fire still stands (No. 435 Hamilton Road) being probably the oldest building within the limits of the modern city of London.

CHAPTER FOUR

CHURCH

And when the builders laid the foundation of the temple of the Lord, they set the priests in their apparel with trumpets, and the Levites the sons of Asaph with cymbals, to praise the Lord, after the ordinance of David King of Israel. And they sang together by course in praising and giving thanks unto the Lord; because he is good, for his mercy endureth for ever toward Israel. And all the people shouted with a great shout, when they praised the Lord, because the foundation of the house of the Lord was laid.

Ezra 3: 10-11

By the middle of November, 1832, life in the village had slid back into its accustomed groove. The first frosts had neutralized the "noxious effluvia" that had caused the cholera epidemic and the first snows had mercifully hidden the unsightly garbage heaps that had promoted its spread.

The population, reduced by dread of the cholera, and increased by the entertainment afforded by the Sovereign hanging, had levelled out at approximately the former figure of some three hundred households.

A number of these households were Anglican. They now had no spiritual solace except what they could provide among themselves, and no shepherd to lead them. Meanwhile the snow drifted about the bare beams of "Boswell's Folly" while moisture and cold went silently ahead with their work of destruction on the uncompleted church.

The SPG had apparently lost some of its interest in the London mission. Perhaps one reason for this was the failure of the congregation even to provide a home for itself. After all, the people of St. Thomas, without the advantages possessed by London as district capital, had constructed a church within a few months of the arrival of their missionary in 1824. If there were special circumstances operating in London they were not obvious to the members of the Society, separated from the scene by an ocean and half a continent.

A field that did excite the interest of the SPG however was the mass migration of settlers from the United Kingdom into the townships west of London the previous summer. This settlement, under distinguished patronage, involved more than two thousand persons many of them presumably with an Established Church background.

The story of this settlement has been adequately and romantically told by one of its literate pioneers and requires no amplification here. Our present interest lies in the fact that Providence manipulated the intent of the SPG into answering the prayers of the London congregation as well.

In August, 1932, as poor, weary Boswell was maintaining his vigil at Blackfriars bridge, a ship sailed from Dublin with a human cargo bound eventually for the Adelaide Township settlement. She was the *Anne of Halifax* and included in her passenger list men and women, boys and girls, destined to leave an imprint on the history of their to-be-adopted land. Three of the families aboard were closely related by marriage —the Cronyns, the Blakes and the Broughs.

It is with the Cronyns that this history is directly concerned and with one member of that family in particular—a young curate, a native of Kilkenny, Ireland, late assistant curate of the parish of Kilcommick, Lislea, County Longford, christened Benjamin.

The Reverend Benjamin Cronyn was on his way to Adelaide Township, whether on his own or with the financial assistance of the SPG is not clear. After a long and difficult sea voyage, six weeks in the quarantine station at Grosse Isle in the St. Lawrence (there had been a death from cholera shortly after the vessel left harbour), additional arduous voyages on two different lake vessels on two different lakes, and a trying thirty-mile ride over a bumpy corduroy road in an ox-cart, Cronyn and his family arrived at the village of London with the prospect of an additional land journey of twenty miles before reaching the Adelaide settlement.

It was night and the roads were perilous even in the daytime. A decision was made to put up at a local hotel for the night. It was a decision which was to prove of prime importance to the congregation of St Paul's and to the present Diocese of Huron.

There were four in the Cronyn family group—the curate,

his wife Margaret, and the two children—Thomas, aged six, and Jane, three. They obtained accommodation at the Mansion House Hotel on Dundas Street, operated by Dr. Hiram Davis Lee, father of Graves Simcoe Lee, whose career was briefly outlined in Chapter Two. London's pioneer innkeeper, Peter MacGregor, had quit the business and the village, heartbroken by the shattering effect of the cholera epidemic on his family circle.

The following day a delegation of London Anglicans waited on the curate. Word of his presence in the village had raised hopes which were dashed to the ground on learning of his destination. However they easily prevailed upon him to preach to them in the schoolhouse. That Sunday in 1832 saw a regular procession of divines utilizing the school for church purposes. A Presbyterian preached in the morning, a Methodist at noon and an Anglican in the afternoon. The Presbyterian cleric, the Reverend William Proudfoot, was another recent arrival.

In his meticulous diary the Presbyterian cleric recorded the events of that day:

Preached to a full house on 1 Thess. 4: 1. . . A Methodist (Mr. Jackson) occupied the place of worship in the middle of the day; and Mr. Cronyn of the Episcopal Church at 4 P.M.

Cronyn's sermon apparently pleased the people for the following day a second, and larger delegation waited on him in an effort to induce him to remain in London. The advantages of London were strongly advanced and the backwoods nature of the Adelaide settlement stressed. The young curate did not take long to arrive at his decision. A third Cronyn was on the way—Verschoyle, born February 6, 1833—and comfortable quarters in a small but thriving village was an attractive proposition. He agreed to the congregation's request, it being understood he would provide care for the settlers of Adelaide as well.

In this casual, apparently accidental way, an association began which was to have far-reaching consequences for the young curate himself and for the congregation whose spiritual welfare he undertook to supervise.

The new missionary rapidly proved himself a man of enormous energy. Within the space of a few weeks he had not only fulfilled his promise to the Adelaide settlers by visiting them and making arrangements for future service but he had also succeeded in making progress in the completion of the London church. In fact Cronyn worked at such feverish speed it is difficult to establish an accurate chronology of events in the first year of his mission.

First of all a committee was organized to complete the church. Three of its members were Lawrence Lawrason, Edward Allen Talbot and Captain Richard Browne. On the instructions of this committee Cronyn visited the government offices in York. The expenses of the trip—£7 10s. Provincial Currency, equal to $30 American—were charged against the building account. The money was put to good use, permission being received to sell the lots on Dundas Street and to use the proceeds to complete the church in a better location. Further, a grant of land was made for the new site. This was the block bounded by North Street (now Queens Avenue), Duke Street (now Dufferin Avenue), Clarence and Richmond streets. The property contained in all four and one-fifth acres.

A gossipy but probably not altogether accurate report of the missionary's visit to York is contained in the diary of the Reverend William Proudfoot under the date, March 7, 1833:

Mr. John Talbot, school-master (brother of Edward Allen Talbot) called. He told me that Mr. Cronyn had returned from York; that the Governor told Mr. Cronyn that Upper Canada will probably be divided and that London will be its capital; that it is his intentions to send respectable loyalist emigrants who may apply to him to its district. . . That it is the intention of the government to raise up such a body of persons attached to the Constitution of Great Britain as may counteract the influence of Yankeeism so prevalent about St. Thomas and along the lake shore. Further that the large Episcopal Church is to be finished this year from funds in the hands of the government.

This last statement was certainly erroneous. The only assistance provided by the government was the land grant, the patent for which was not officially issued until January 18, 1836, when the parish was formally constituted by the Crown.

Sometime during the winter of 1832/33 the frame built under Boswell's direction was moved from the corner of Dundas and Ridout Streets to its new location. This was accomplished by a contractor, Lewis Hartman, who mounted the frame on sleighs and dragged it three city blocks with teams of oxen. His fee was £25 ($100).

Hartman also received the contract for the building of the new church. He began work about May 1, 1833, and submitted his last statement to the building committee on December 4 of the same year. The total cost of the church was £862 14s. 5½d. Provincial Currency ($3,451). According to the accounts for the building to be seen among the Cronyn Papers at Huron College, London, Edward Allen Talbot undertook to clear the old site (£3 15s.); John Jennings cleared the new site (£8 9s. 3½d.); William Hale provided the bricks for the foundation (£3); Dennis O'Brien hauled the materials (£10); William Haskett provided the labour (£36 5s.); Charles Sifton dug the eighteen-foot well (£5 18s. 9d.) and Robert Green supplied the pumps (£2 1s. 3d.). Hartman's total bill, including the charge for moving the frame, was £675.

This was quite a notable effort on the part of a small congregation. However the costs were more than covered by the sale of the old site. Broken up into building lots the property fetched a total of £877 4s. 1½d. ($3,509). In addition to this amount a stranger subscribed £1 5s. ($5) to the building fund.

The purchasers of the lots, most of them village merchants, were: George J. Goodhue, Dennis O'Brien, Mr. Lyman, Mr. Hunt, Mr. Schwieger, Messrs. Parks, Messrs. Robertson and the Reverend Benjamin Cronyn himself. Dennis O'Brien shortly afterwards built on his lot the first brick building in the village.

There is considerable confusion in the records as to the date of the opening of the new church. From various references it would appear that the church was actually in use before the building program was completed and certainly prior to the official date of opening. For instance on Thursday, February 14, 1833, the date officially set aside by the government for province-wide services of thanksgiving for the passing

of the cholera epidemic, the Reverend William Proudfoot
records in his diary:

Though this is the Fast Day or Thanksgiving Day, I saw no
symptoms of its being kept. There was service in the English
Church. . .

Again on March 10 there is reference to the church as well
as an unflattering reference to its parson:

On this morning I attended the Episcopal Church. Mr. Cronyn
preached a miserable but an orthodox sermon on the whole
Christian armour. It beggared all description, but he seemed a
serious man and sound in the faith so far as he knows anything
about it.

In addition there is a notation in Cronyn's report to the
SPG on January 5, 1833, referring to the new church, com-
menting parenthetically that "until within the last three
months we met in the seminary (the schoolhouse). Three
days after this date a wedding was performed, possibly in the
church, vividly recalled sixty-nine years later by one of the
participants:

On the 8th day of January, 1833, your father married Freeman
Talbot and Ann Eliza Clark, the first couple ever married by
your father in Canada, as you will see by the records today in
St. Paul's Cathedral.

From other references it is apparent that Cronyn's congregation was still using the schoolhouse for services. Under
date of August 3, 1833, Proudfoot complains that Cronyn had
"deranged our system in regard to occupying the schoolhouse." Something over a month later insult was added to
injury when the Presbyterian cleric showed up for his appointed turn at using the building to find the Church of
England man preaching to his congregation. The Presby-
terians proved to be bears for punishment. They all returned
in the afternoon when Proudfoot delivered a lecture on the
first six verses of the Epistle of St. Paul to the Galatians. The
sixth verse seemed under the circumstances particularly per-
tinent: "I marvel that ye are so soon removed from him that
called you into the grace of Christ unto another Gospel."

From these and other references it looks as if the new church, although unfinished, was occasionally used for special services, with regular services continuing to be held in the schoolhouse. By the end of the year the church interior was sufficiently in order to hold the Christmas communion there, at which time there were thirty communicants.

The formal opening of St. Paul's, according to the Proudfoot diary, took place on September 14, 1834. No newspaper account survives so we are left to speculate at the nature of the ceremonies attending the opening. Edward Allen Talbot's paper, The Sun, had succumbed to financial pressures sometime in 1833. Its place had been taken by The True Patriot, edited and published by Colonel George Washington Busteed. The Patriot flourished only a short time and the Colonel, who had once been secretary to the governor of the West Indies, returned to New York where he engaged in merchandising a patented soap guaranteed to cure most of the ills known to man. A few copies of The Patriot survive; none has yet been found of The Sun.

In the absence of contemporary accounts, the interior and exterior appearance of the new St. Paul's Church has to be pieced together from a few scattered reminiscences and one picture painted in the 1840's in which the church appears to one side, rearing a rather extraordinary square tower above the rail fences, stumps and outhouses which then cluttered downtown London.

The church faced south on to North Street (the present Queens Avenue). It was of wood construction like all the other buildings in the village with the sole exception of the courthouse. The tower or spire was too large in proportion to the church, as most observers pointed out. Considering the population of the village it was a large church with a seating capacity of 400 and yet within a very few years Cronyn was reporting that the average number in attendance on Sunday was 420.

Such was the first Church of St. Paul. From the erection of the frame in the summer of 1830 it had taken four years to build. Unlike most modern parish churches it began its service to the community free of all debt, thanks to the business acumen of the Reverend Benjamin Cronyn.

Cronyn's position in London was regularized by Bishop Stewart on May 6, 1833, when he was appointed to the cure of souls in the town and township of London. At the same time the bishop wrote to Richard Browne, a member of the building committee and an acting churchwarden, urging the friends of the church "to make such addition to Mr. Cronyn's income . . . as may enable him to dwell amongst them in that proper comfort which is his due."

In the following February nine members of the London church, describing themselves as "duly elected members of the Select Vestry of the Township of London in the Province of Upper Canada" agreed to serve as agents for the collection of funds towards the support of their parson. The document, to be found in the Cronyn Papers at Huron College, London, is the earliest record of a formal church organization at St. Paul's. The nine signatories, all persons of consequence in the tiny village were: Lawrence Lawrason, a prominent general merchant and the second of that name to be a member of the congregation; John Kent, a gentleman farmer and pioneer real estate developer; George Kennedy, of whom nothing seems to be known; John B. (for Baptiste) Askin, clerk of the peace for the District of London; Richard Browne, gentleman; William Haskett, farmer and one of the sub-contractors for the building of the church; J. Parkinson, farmer; Hiram Davis Lee, physician and hotel proprietor; and John Hawkins, schoolmaster.

CHAPTER FIVE

FIRE

And there came a fire out from before the Lord, and consumed upon the altar the burnt offering and the fat; which when all the people saw, they shouted, and fell on their faces.

Leviticus 9: 24

The tall-towered first Church of St. Paul served its community for a few short months short of ten years. For the church, its rector, its congregation and its parish, these were years filled with excitement and high drama.

The curtain-raiser was the critical provincial election of 1836 in which Benjamin Cronyn played an active role. Four years' residence in Upper Canada had given him sufficient knowledge of the country, the people and the political situation to place him in a position of some influence.

That knowledge had been gained at first-hand on the back roads and in the backwoods. In his report to Bishop Stewart in January, 1835, Cronyn listed the congregations to which he was ministering. His congregation in London (St. Paul's) consisted of some two hundred persons; a second in London Township (St. John's, Arva) consisted of one hundred and fifty people; and a third, also in the township, eleven miles north of London, consisted of three hundred persons.

In addition to serving these three parishes, Cronyn interested himself actively in the work of the Church throughout the area, becoming deeply involved in the formation and work of the Western Clerical Society, organized to promote the interests of the church in the western counties.

His position in his adopted community was raised considerably in importance in 1836 when St. Paul's became one

37

of forty-four rectories established by the Crown on the recommendation of the Lieutenant-Governor of Upper Canada, Sir John Colborne.

It was perhaps inevitable that the rector of St. Paul's should become implicated in the political issues which were shortly to erupt in armed revolt. The Church of England was so thoroughly involved in those issues that no parson of any spirit could remain aloof from them. And Cronyn had spirit.

Almost from the day of his arrival in Canada Benjamin Cronyn showed a personal and practical interest in the land dealings of his Church. By the Canada Act of 1791 a reserve of land in each new township, equal to one-seventh of the land granted to individuals, had been set aside for the support of "a Protestant clergy." From the beginning the Church of England had assumed itself to be the object of this legislative benefice. The supporters of the other churches challenged the assumption. In the result, with the support of a largely Anglican and Tory ruling class, the lion's share of the Clergy Reserves went to the Church of England. By 1833 the Church of England had received 22,345 acres; the "Kirk of Scotland," 1,160; and the Roman Catholic Church, 400 acres. The other churches including the Methodists (numerically the strongest group) received nothing at all.

This is not the place for a detailed study of Benjamin Cronyn's land dealings in his own behalf and that of his Church. Suffice it to say that he proved himself a shrewd businessman and neither he nor his Church suffered as a result.

One of the principal objections to the Clergy Reserve grants was that the presence of these unimproved, uncleared lots impeded settlement and the building of roads. As immigration increased in the 1830's so did the resentment against the Reserves and their beneficiary.

The Reform Party, under the leadership of William Lyon Mackenzie, fanned this resentment into open flame. It became finally an unabashed class struggle—the privileged, as represented by the Tories, their leaders, the so-called Family Compact, and their Church versus the underprivileged individuals and churches.

It has been said that if the Reform Party had won the election of 1836 there would have been no rebellion in Upper Canada. Whatever the truth of this statement it is certain that the bitterness engendered by the tactics used by the Tories on that occasion was a contributing factor in precipitating the uprising.

The little village of London was a particular storm centre in the election. With a population hovering around the one-thousand mark and a strongly-entrenched "little Family Compact" of its own, it was set up as a separate riding in the hope it would provide a safe seat for the Tory nominee, Lieutenant-Colonel Mahlon Burwell, a surveyor, an extensive landowner and a close associate of Lieutenant-Colonel Thomas Talbot. The Reformers nominated John Scatcherd, a local farmer.

The London Tories threw everything they had into the election—including Benjamin Cronyn. The Reverend William Proudfoot who had strong Reform sympathies records his attitude towards Cronyn's activities in a curt diary entry under the date of June 23, 1836:

Parson Cronyn has been all over the Township electioneering. Bah!

The Tories did not have it all their own way. The Reformers showed surprising strength in the town and the surrounding area. Tempers mounted to fever heat as the day of the election—July 1, 1836—approached. The election itself was a disgrace to democratic institutions. No local newspaper files survive for the period but there is sufficient other evidence to prove that the Tories won the election by methods which would today call for an immediate Royal Commission. As it was, the charges against the local Tories were of a sufficiently serious nature to warrant investigation by a Select Committee of the Tory-dominated Legislative Assembly.

Several of the eyewitnesses of the events of that day place Benjamin Cronyn and some of his leading parishioners in the thick of the fray. Robert Davis a local farmer who later lost his life fighting for the Reform cause described the melee in these words:

If you had been in London at the last election, you would have seen a set of government tools called Orange men, running up and down the streets crying five pounds for a liberal; and if a man said a word contrary to their opinion he was knocked down. Many were knocked down in this way and others threatened; and all this in the presence of magistrates, Church of England ministers and judges, who made use of no means to prevent such outrages.

Another admittedly-biased eyewitness was Dr. Charles Duncombe, one of the members for Oxford County, and himself a leader of the Rebellion of 1837. Duncombe, in a memorial addressed to the British Government, claimed that on the day of the election as he approached London he met a Reform candidate, Elias Moore, running for his life from Tory Orangemen and that in London itself he found Reformers being driven away from the polls by armed Tories. This, he said, was done in the presence of officers of the law and of the "rector of the endowed Church of England parish."

A more objective account by a visitor to London fails to identify any of the participants but characterizes the affair as a "gathering which for riot and drunkenness . . . exceeded everything he had ever seen before."

Most of the accounts coupled the name of the rector's warden, Lawrence Lawrason, with that of Cronyn as one of the principals on that disgraceful day. Both were summoned to appear before the Select Committee and their evidence substantially agreed. The rector admitted that there had been violence but said he had often seen more fighting on the annual militia training day. This may well have been so for training day, which occurred on June 4 each year, was notoriously an occasion for excess.

Cronyn's participation in the exciting events of election day was physically passive. His brother Thomas on the other hand was apparently not content with words. An old record reports that Edward Grattan, printer and publisher of *The London Times* was held on bonds "to give evidence against Thomas Cronyn, indicted for assault."

The results of the investigation by the Select Committee were inconclusive and unsatisfactory to both parties. Within a few months the extremists among the Reformers had taken steps to implement their grievances by force of arms.

Benjamin Cronyn missed most of the excitement of that year of decision. In January he and the Reverend William Bettridge of Woodstock left for England to seek financial support for the church in Upper Canada .They went as official representatives and officers of the Western Clerical Society, of which Cronyn was chairman and Bettridge, secretary.

The Reverend Thomas Greene, a young graduate (age twenty-seven) of Trinity College, Dublin, took charge of St. Paul's during Cronyn's absence. Greene had been licensed by Bishop Stewart as a travelling missionary in the District of London in January, 1836.

Greene baptized four children on March 2, 1837, the first entries in St. Paul's register under his name. History was still repeating itself. As in the case of Boswell and Cronyn before him these entries record vital statistics relative to the Tipperary Irish settlers of London Township, brought to the New World in 1818 by Richard S. Talbot.

Greene was in the process of becoming a vital statistic himself. On September 22, 1837, while the village was vibrating like an overstrung violin with rumours of rebellion, the Reverend Thomas Greene was married to an Irish girl, Kate Jane Cruma Killaly, by the Reverend Richard Flood, of the village of Delaware.

Miss Killaly was the daughter of Hamilton H. Killaly, a transplanted Irish squire of the Regency variety. Killaly stalks through the history of the region like a small-screen version of the Prince Regent himself. Like George the Fourth he was sartorially colourful and his appetites were immense. On being charged on one occasion with the amount of drunkenness he permitted to the guests at his home "Fanshawe" (named for the family's estate in Ireland), he replied that he had never seen anyone drunk in his home. Being an honest man, he was forced to add in explanation of this extraordinary statement that he himself was always the first under the table.

Despite these amiable shortcomings, Hamilton Killaly gave much to his adopted country. As the first minister of public works he was responsible for developing the road system of the province which, prior to the coming of the railways in the 1850's, was considered one of the best on the continent.

Judging from the gap in the church records from September 22 to October 23, 1837, Killaly's new son-in-law and his bride enjoyed a short honeymoon before red ruin descended on the village.

The full story of the Rebellion of 1837 as it affected the village of London has yet to be written. The clandestine meetings, the secret passwords, the spy system, the hidden caches of ammunition—this is the material of romance, but this is not the place to tell the tale.

With few exceptions the congregation of St. Paul's remained loyal to the government of Upper Canada. To them the whole thing was ugly and dangerous and the rebels were villains, fit only for hanging. The rebels were the romanticists and they wrote their history on the run, and little of it.

The rebel movement in the District of London was large, powerful and well-supported but the collapse of William Lyon Mackenzie's ill-trained force at Montgomery's Tavern in Toronto on December 7 left them isolated and at the mercy of swift-moving militia. Dr. Charles Duncombe, of St. Thomas, leader of the western forces, decided against resistance and disbanded his troops at the village of Scotland, in Brant County, a few days later.

Then the witch-hunt began. By the end of the year hundreds of suspected rebels had been arrested and confined in the London jail for varying periods, often without even the formal laying of charges. The prisoners came from all classes of the community. There were storekeepers and farmers and cattle-drovers and ironmongers. John Talbot, son of Richard Talbot and a parishioner of St. Paul's, fled for his life to the United States with a price on his head and his brother Edward Allen, the writer and editor, was arrested on suspicion.

Suspicion was, in fact the great enemy of the people. Rumours flew wildly in every direction. Typical of the state of mind of the inhabitants is the story told in later years by Colonel L. A. Norton, of California, himself deeply implicated in the Rebellion:

I learned that Colonel Maitland of the 32nd Infantry, then guard-
ing London, was to march down to Delaware, while another
command, with military stores, was to reach London next morning.
I learned that after Colonel Maitland left, only 30 raw recruits
would hold the village and devised the plan of having my uncle
David assemble the Scotch on Westminster Street, make a night
attack, release the prisoners and capture London. At this time my
uncles were at the head of 400 Patriots, but they could not do
anything toward carrying out the plans. The village was in a
fever. Scouts were sent out but were afraid to go out of sight of the
settlement. They would retire to some secluded place, and ride
their horses until they would get them in a perfect foam; then
come rushing in and report the rebels surrounding all sides of the
Union. Another would come in and report them nearer. At last
they got them within three miles of the town, when Hughey (or
Howie), the Turnkey came in the room where the prisoners were,
saying "I would give $100 for an axe to cut down the bridge." The
rebels had taken or hidden all the axes. People were hastily
packing up and leaving . . .

This, like all the other alarms, was false, but the people
were ready to believe them all. Their fears were somewhat
alleviated by the arrival of a battalion of the 32nd Regiment
of Foot under the command of Lieutenant-Colonel John
Maitland, mentioned in the excerpt above. Maitland, a son
of the Earl of Lauderdale, was a half-mad little martinet who
exercised the brutal regulations of the British Army of that
period with savage satisfaction. On one occasion, dissatisfied
with the manner in which lashes were being applied to the
back of an offending private, he snatched the whip from the
hands of the person administering the punishment and completed the job his own way. The man died. On another
occasion, carrying out the full prescribed penalty, he sentenced
a man who had deserted his post to fifty lashes, branding with
the letter "D" on both palms and transportation to the penal
colony of Van Diemen's Land (Tasmania) for life.

This was London's "protector" and London had soon had
enough of him. When he died, quite suddenly, in 1839, he
was given the largest and most impressive funeral the village
had ever seen—and the happiest. He was buried on the
grounds of St. Paul's but the location of the grave and the
stone that was supposed to have marked it has been lost.

For nearly two years following the collapse of the Mackenzie revolt the people of London lived in a state of almost hourly panic. The leaders of the rebellion, most of whom escaped to the United States, organized a rag-tag army of unemployed young Americans who, as self-styled Patriots, terrorized the border communities of Upper Canada from Windsor to Prescott. Throughout 1838 they made several raids, all unsuccessful. The last attack in the western counties came on December 4 when a band of more than one hundred Patriots crossed the Detroit river to Windsor. In a short but savage encounter with the Canadian militia, the invaders suffered heavy casualties, a number being killed and wounded and forty-four taken prisoner.

The prisoners were hauled to London and lodged in the already overcrowded jail. In a swift trial by court-martial, forty-three of the forty-four were found guilty and sentenced to death. Six men were actually hanged in the courthouse square during the early part of January. An additional sixteen were transported to Van Diemen's Land and the rest were deported to the United States.

Cronyn family tradition records that the rector of St. Paul's attended the six condemned men at the gallows. It is said he found the experience "harrowing" and felt that the sentences were unduly harsh.

The Reverend Thomas Greene, Cronyn's erstwhile surrogate was apparently of a less forgiving nature. About this time he wrote a letter to the editor of *The London* (Canada) *Times*, roundly condemning the Protestant churches for adding fuel to the fire of rebellion, and expressing belief that not one member of the Church of England was known to have participated in the revolt. His letter concluded with this extraordinarily partisan statement:

We see who are the disaffected, and who are the contented. How desirable then by every means to increase the number of the latter and draw off from the ranks of the former. In a word, how all-important is it for the promotion of good order and peace in Upper Canada to look well to the provision existing for the sound religious instruction of the people there in the principles of the Church of England. Can it be doubted that the efficiency of the

Church in Canada is important towards quelling existing disorders and promoting a healthier tone of society, harmony among the inhabitants and obedience to the laws? In the disaffected parts of Upper Canada it is evident it must be available to this end.

The letter was reprinted in *The Church*, the official organ of the Church of England in Upper Canada, and precipitated an avalanche of criticism from the other church groups in the province.

One aftermath of the Rebellion permanently affected the life of the village of London. That was the establishment of a garrison of British troops. Temporary accommodation in a number of downtown buildings was soon exchanged for a permanent barracks somewhat to the north, on land now occupied by Victoria Park. The complex of buildings, some of log, some framed structures, took some years to erect. The contractor was a prominent member of St. Paul's Church, Edward Matthews. The contract, by far the largest granted in London up to this time, involved more than one hundred thousand pounds. Like many another before him, and since, Matthews found financing such a project eventually an intolerable burden. He later became inextricably enmeshed in land speculation and died a suicide on June 22, 1851. Memorial tablets to the memory of his young wife and three of his children are to be seen in the north transept of the Cathedral. There is no memorial to the contractor himself.

As soon as the intention of the British government to make London a garrison town became known, Cronyn applied for the chaplaincy of the barracks, which he obtained. Church parades became a regular and colourful addition to the life of St. Paul's. The presence of the military also contributed handsomely to the coffers of the church. The entry in the Preacher's Book for June 9, 1839, for instance, records a civilian collection of 12s. 6d., while £3 15s. 7½d. was collected from the military.

With the passing of the rebellion and its attendant excitement, life in London and at St. Paul's settled down into more normal patterns. The church which had seemed more than adequate for the needs of its congregation in 1834 was beginning to be overcrowded six years later. Average attendance seems to have hovered near the four hundred mark, with up to eighty-five receiving the sacrament at the infrequent communion services (normally four in a year).

The town was growing. In January, it achieved the status of a police village. At the first municipal election George Jervis Goodhue, a member of the congregation of St. Paul's, became president of the village board. Goodhue, a tall Connecticut Yankee with cold blue eyes, was London's first merchant. He operated his business with such cool efficiency that in the year of his election to chief office he retired from merchandising and entered the even more lucrative field of land speculation. By his death in 1870 he had put together a personal fortune in excess of one million dollars.

It is of incidental interest to note that of the seven presidents who headed the board during London's village days, six were members of St. Paul's congregation. In addition to Goodhue they were: James Givens, a leading barrister, president in 1841; Edward Matthews, the unhappy contractor, 1842-43; John Balkwill, a pioneer brewer who established in 1828 what later became the brewery of John Labatt, Limited, president in 1845; T. W. Shepherd, 1846; and Dr. Hiram Davis Lee, physician and hotel-keeper, president in 1847.

James Givens and T. W. Shepherd led relatively quiet lives; the same could not be said for the other Anglican presidents of the village board. Goodhue's single-minded financial career made him one of the most disliked public figures in Ontario; the sad story of Edward Matthews has already been told; Dr. Lee, in addition to being the father of a brilliant actor (Graves Simcoe Lee, briefly mentioned in Chapter Two) was a notable village character in his own right. In this day of medical specialization, Lee's dual career may seem faintly comic, but in the early days of settlement in Upper Canada, many professional men were obliged to "double in brass" to keep body and soul together. Doctors were all too often paid in produce, if at all, while no one expected a tavern-keeper to accept anything but cash. Even so, there were occasional comments about Lee's economically-split personality. A piece of very bad satirical verse on the brief hotel career of one

Peter McCann, which appeared in *The London* (Canada) *Times* of January 23, 1846, makes oblique reference to Dr. Lee:

He (McCann) had five beds and a bunk,
But says Lee's he will get drunk,
You cannot tell just how he feels,
For he buys no more "Lee's pills".

The good doctor, last presiding officer of the village board died before his term of office was up, a victim of the ship's fever epidemic of 1847.

John Balkwill was a merry rogue who frequently over-indulged in the product of his own brewery, as the minutes of the village board meeting of October 23, 1843, plainly testify:

John Balkwill, Esq. having attended the Board in a state of intoxication: ordered, that the constable do remove him; he having done everything in his power to impede the proceedings of the Board.
John Balkwill, Esq., one of the members of the Board, having broken the windows of the office, or instigated the same to be done; ordered, that the Board adjourn till tomorrow morning.

As a result of Balkwill's merry pranks the village clerk, William King Cornish, threatened to resign. Considering the fact that Cornish, in addition to siring that extraordinary politician, Frank Cornish, was given to other practical jokes as well (one of which cost him his lawyer's gown) the behaviour of the brewer must have been extravagantly outrageous on this occasion to warrant such action.

In these conformist days few villages can boast more than one or two "characters"; London in the 1840's could have supplied a hundred, and of the hundred at least seventy-five would have been Anglicans.

The church could use them today.

Mention has already been made of the overcrowding at St. Paul's, due largely to the addition of the military to the regular congregation. Steps were taken in the latter part of 1843 to alleviate this situation by the addition of galleries. Donations were sought for this purpose and the sum of £50 Provincial Currency ($200) had been raised by the beginning of the Lenten season of 1844.

The church faced a reasonably prosperous future even if it had no linens, as Cronyn's report for 1840 complains. (Apparently some lady of the congregation supplied a cloth for the Communion Table and a napkin to cover the elements each time the Sacrament was administered.) The building was paid for, the four hundred acres of glebe land belonging to the parish was under cultivation and rented and the congregation was affluent enough to provide a special yearly collection of four to five pounds for the alleviation of the suffering of the poor within the parish limits. From the post-rebellion period onwards through the long history of St. Paul's a concern for the distressed within its reach has been a constant feature of the church's witness, culminating with the unique Core Area Project inaugurated in the fall of 1963.

The musical life of the church had not been overlooked. Early in 1844 an organ was installed. The instrument was the unaided work of George Pringle, a village cabinetmaker. There is no way of telling how good the organ was. It was heard only on two or three public occasions and those who heard left no record of its excellence or otherwise.

The hand of God fell upon St. Paul's on the first day of Lent, 1844. On February 21, Ash Wednesday, the church caught fire and burned to the ground.

No complete newspaper files for the period survive, so it is impossible to relate exactly what happened, although from one or two references it would appear the burning church ignited some other buildings to the south of it.

The collapse of the ungainly spire, the whine of the flames through the pipes of George Pringle's organ, the crumbling into ashes of the frame laboriously erected under Edward Boswell's direction in the summer of 1830—all went unrecorded. All that was remembered, to be set down many years later, was the mighty fall of the brand-new bell, only recently installed in the steeple. With a vast, complaining, musical crash, it fell to the ground and its fall was heard and lamented within the square mile of the parish bounds.

NOTE: The Rebellion documents quoted in this chapter are from *Western Ontario and the American Frontier* by Fred Landon. (The Ryerson Press, Toronto: 1941).

CHAPTER SIX

PHOENIX

*The Spirit of the Lord God is upon me; because the Lord hath
anointed me to preach good tidings unto the meek . . . to appoint
unto them that mourn in Zion, to give unto them beauty for
ashes, the oil of joy for mourning, the garment of praise for the
spirit of heaviness; that they might be called trees of righteousness,
the planting of the Lord, that he might be glorified.*

Isaiah 61: 1-3

The congregation of St. Paul's was shocked but not de-
moralized by the tragedy that had struck the church. There
was no service on Sunday, February 25, but by the following
Sunday arrangements had been made for the use of the
Mechanics' Institute building on the courthouse square.

The Institute, a small neat building with a classical portico,
had been built three years previously to serve the community
as a library and reading room, with facilities also for lectures
and public meetings. Mechanics' Institutes were being
founded in all the larger towns in the province in the 1840's.
They were based on an English model and represented a
nineteenth century adult education movement. The London
Mechanics' Institute eventually developed into a public
library system.

The auditorium of the Institute must have been of reasonable size for at the Easter Communion on April 7, Benjamin
Cronyn administered the sacrament to eighty-five communicants, who would not of course represent the total congregation present on that occasion.

On the Friday following the first service in the Institute,
that is on March 8, 1844, a special meeting of the vestry
of St. Paul's was held at William Balkwill's tavern to lay
plans for the building of a new church. The first resolution
outlined the intended dimensions and general form of the
new building:

49

Moved by John Wilson Esqr. and seconded by the Honble. Geo. J. Goodhue: "That St. Paul's Church about to be built on the site of the one lately consumed shall be Brick on a Stone foundation, about Sixty feet by Ninety inside the walls, varying not more than ten feet either way in the discretion of the Building Committee to be hereafter appointed for the erection of said Church, which shall be Gothic in its Architecture."

The second resolution named the building committee, consisting of the following gentlemen: John Wilson, C. S. Gzowski, Francis Pope, Edward Matthews, William W. Street, Geo. J. Goodhue, George Thomas, William Till, Thomas Worthington and Samuel Peters.

Here once again we see associated with St. Paul's the names of community leaders, men whose peculiar talents and often extraordinary careers demonstrate vividly the type of brilliant nonconformist who laid Canada's urban foundations and whose departure from the Canadian scene left our cities so sadly depleted of individualism.

Edward Matthews and George J. Goodhue we already know about. William Warren Street was auditor of the district of London and manager of the Gore Bank on Ridout Street. William Till was a cabinetmaker, Thomas Worthington a plumber, and Francis Pope a general contractor. Judging from his copperplate handwriting George Thomas, secretary of the committee, was probably a professional man of some kind.

Samuel Peters, a pioneer surveyor and distiller prominent in the Masonic Order, built a large home to the west of the original townsite overlooking London. The village that grew up in the vicinity was known as Petersville in his honour and retained that name until annexed to the city in 1896. The Peters' home still stands and is occupied by Samuel Peters' granddaughter, Mrs. James P. Dunn, who is a member of the Cathedral congregation.

Casimir Stanislaus Gzowski (later Sir Casimir) was born in St. Petersburg, Russia, in 1813, a son of Stanislaw, Count Gzowski, a Polish officer in the Imperial Russian Guard. Gzowski studied military engineering in Poland and entered the Russian army. However in November, 1830, he took part in an abortive Polish uprising against the Czar and was wounded, captured, imprisoned and later exiled. He arrived in New York City in 1833 and after eight years there removed to Upper Canada, settling in London. He became chief engineer of the provincial department of public works under his fellow-townsman, Hamilton H. Killaly. In 1853 he organized the firm of Gzowski and Company, which secured the contract for the building of the Grand Trunk Railway from Toronto to Sarnia. A later and more famous achievement of the company was the building of the International Bridge at Niagara Falls in 1871-1873. Gzowski was knighted by Queen Victoria in 1890 and died in Toronto in 1898.

Even in such illustrious company, the career of John Wilson, chairman of the building committee for the new St. Paul's, must be adjudged extraordinary. Wilson, a pioneer London lawyer of Scottish birth, was the surviving participant of the last fatal duel to be fought in Canada. In June, 1833, at dawn on the banks of the River Tay, near Perth, Upper Canada, he met a fellow law-student, Robert Lyon and, in a double exchange of shots, fatally wounded his opponent. At the subsequent trial in Brockville Wilson defended himself and won an acquittal. This terse review scarcely does credit to an incident heavily overlaid with Victorian romanticism. The cause of the dispute between the two friends was the honourable name of a young lady, whom Wilson later married. There was even a villain in the piece, rejoicing in the richly evil name of Lelievre.

The victorious duelist came to London in 1834 where he rapidly established an outstanding reputation as a jurist, politician and philanthropist. He first entered politics in 1847, winning the London riding as a Reform candidate. A derogatory remark made in Parliament about the Irish caused him to lose his seat in 1851 to a fellow member of St. Paul's, Thomas C. Dixon, a Tory hatter.

"Honest John" Wilson, one of the most popular politicians ever to seek office in London, was in and out of the Parliamentary scene until 1857 when he withdrew his name from candidacy. He was elevated to the bench in 1863, serving as a judge until his death in 1869.

These then were the men who assumed the responsibility for building the new St. Paul's Church. Before Easter, 1844, they had accepted a plan prepared by William Thomas, a Toronto architect.

Thomas was a native of Stroud, Gloucestershire, England, where he was born in 1800. After practising as an architect at Leamington, where he designed Lansdowne Crescent and Circus, he emigrated to Canada and settled in Toronto, where he designed both St. Michael's Roman Catholic Cathedral and the jail.

The late Reverend Dr. A. H. Crowfoot, biographer of Benjamin Cronyn, drew attention to the similarity between the tower Thomas designed for St. Paul's, London, and the tower that Sir Charles Barry, architect of the British Houses of Parliament, designed for St. Peter's, Brighton, and suggested that William Thomas may have been a pupil of the great Englishman.

Dr. Crowfoot also is authority for the statement that the stone used in the building of the Canadian church was from the same quarries on Portland Bill as the stone used by Christopher Wren in the erection of St. Paul's Cathedral in London, England.

William Thomas' plan for St. Paul's called for a building with inside dimensions of 59 feet in width and 85 feet in length. There were no transepts and the chancel was to be a "half octagon of 31 feet in breadth and 15 feet 6 inches in depth." The tower was to be built of "sufficient size and strength to receive a peal of Six Bells".

The estimated cost of the structure was approximately £4,000 ($16,000). In the result the figure was closer to £7,000. Partially offsetting this large outlay was the insurance carried on the former building. This, according to the treasurer's accounts, amounted to £1,000, the proceeds of two policies— one for £800, carried by the "Alliance Office"; the second, for £200, by the "Buffalo Company".

Unfortunately for George Pringle, the talented cabinet-maker, the insurance policies did not cover his labouriously handmade organ. Pringle applied to the vestry of St. Paul's for compensation for the loss of the instrument. The members of the vestry rather brutally declined to take any responsibility for a piece of equipment which they had neither commissioned nor agreed to purchase. Pringle apparently refused to give up his claim and after five years of internal haggling, someone gave authority to the treasurer to settle the amount, in October, 1849, with a payment of £17 10s.

The building committee moved ahead swiftly with its plans and the laying of the cornerstone took place on the feast of the Nativity of St. John the Baptist, June 24, 1844.

The Right Reverend John Strachan, Lord Bishop of Toronto in whose diocese the church was situated, came to London especially for the occasion, which he later reported to the Society for the Promotion of Christian Knowledge, in England, was "quite a holy day in the town".

The bishop's description of the mood of the community is fully warranted by the report of the event which appeared originally in *The London Inquirer* and later reprinted in *The Church* of July 5. The account reads, in part:

We are always glad to mark the progress of improvement and we are glad to record an event, that while it is likely to contribute to the architectural beauty of our town, will in moral point of view, be attended with more signal results. We allude to the erection of a new Episcopal Church on the site where the old one stood. The laying of the foundation stone of this building took place on Monday last, with Masonic honors, and we will venture to say a more imposing and interesting display has never been witnessed in our town. The intended ceremony having been duly announced, crowds from the surrounding country met to witness it, and accordingly at an early hour our streets were thronged with anxious spectators, and presented a gay and animated aspect. The proceedings were well and judiciously arranged, and luckily the favorable state of the weather gave everyone an opportunity of enjoying the occasion.

The Lord Bishop of Toronto came to London expressly for the purpose of affording his assistance and sanction, and all classes and denominations joined in a truly Christian spirit to do honour to the occasion. Never have we seen a more numerous and respectable procession in this town, and never has any public ceremony passed off with greater éclat.

William Niles one of the founders of Freemasonry in London was marshal of the day. The procession assembled at the

Middlesex County courthouse where a service was conducted by the Reverend Benjamin Cronyn. The procession then paraded through the streets of the town to the site of the new church. The parade order was as follows:

W. Thomas, the architect, a Union Jack, the town band, drums and fifes of the 23rd Royal Welch Fusiliers, tyler of Lodge No. 209, under whose auspices the stone was being laid, the bishop of Toronto, supported on the right by Wilson Mills, chaplain of St. John's Lodge, and on the left by Rev. Benjamin Cronyn, rector of the church. Clergy followed in their robes and then a Masonic banner, stewards, the master and members of St. John's Lodge, two by two.

After the lodge members went the sheriff of the London district, the judge of the London district court, the clerk of the peace, the members of the bar in their robes, the church wardens, the president and members of the Mechanics' Institute of London, with their flag, the president and members of St. George's Society of St. Thomas, with their banners, the president and members of St. George's Society of London, also with their banners, as well as the members of both St. Andrew's and St. Patrick's Societies of London with their banners. The end of the procession was brought up by "citizens of the Town of London and neighbourhood". Just what citizens were in the parade is not said.

In this order the procession moved to St. Paul's churchyard where, in the presence of several thousand spectators the laying of the foundation stone took place. Bishop Strachan presided and Samuel Peters, Worshipful Master of St. John's Lodge Number 209 (a) wielded the silver trowel, repeating the ancient words:

In the faith of Jesus Christ we lay this foundation stone in the name of God the Father, God the Son, and God the Holy Ghost. *Amen.*

The trowel used on this occasion is today the property of Samuel Peters' granddaughter, Mrs. James P. Dunn, of Grosvenor Lodge.

According to *The Inquirer* account, the "amateur band" of London deserved much credit for the manner in which they acquitted themselves on the occasion, and the inspiring anthems sung added much to the harmony and solemnity.

Two parchment inscriptions, "beautifully drawn and printed by Mr. Robert M. Moore, surveyor and draftsman, of this town" along with other things, were deposited in the stone. The first was a Masonic inscription, "St. John's Lodge, No. 209, held at London, C.W., under the sanction of the Grand Lodge of Ireland, this corner stone was laid on Monday, the 24th of June, 1844, and of Masonry 5844. With Masonic honours, being the anniversary of St. John the Baptist. Samuel Peters, worshipful master, *pro tem*, acting on behalf of Hugh Falconer, W.M." A list of the officers of the year followed.

The second parchment gave the year and also the year of the reign of Queen Victoria along with all her titles. Then followed the names of the governor-general; the bishop, the rector, and the two wardens, Lawrence Lawrason, M.P.P., and William W. Street. The architect's name, William Thomas, completed the list. The inscription concluded with some information regarding the previous church. "This church was erected upon the site of one built of wood in 1833 and destroyed by fire on Ash Wednesday, February 21, 1844."

In addition to the parchments, the stone contained silver coins, numbers of the church newspaper, *The Ecclesiastical Gazette*, *The Inquirer* and *The Patriot*, portraits of the Queen, the governor-general, the chief justice and Colonel Talbot. Why a prize list of Upper Canada College was also included is not explained.

The evening ended up with a Masonic banquet at which, in the custom of the day, endless toasts were proposed and responded to with increasing fluency and decreasing coherency.

Once the celebration was over the work of letting tenders for the building proceeded with redoubled energy. At a meeting of the building committee on July 18 the following tenders were accepted:

For the stone work, Henry Simpson, of Toronto, £636; bricklaying and plastering, Buckle and Robinson, London, £675; plumbing and glazing, Thomas Worthington, London, £132 10s.; painting J. Bonser and Thomas Fletcher, both of

London, £100. The carpentry and joiners' work, the largest contract, was let to Messrs. Pope and Till of London, after some haggling, at £1,050.

The total amount of the contracts was £2,593 10s. The cautious Mr. Goodhue raised a formal objection to proceeding with the building without having sufficient funds in hand, "as he considers that . . . the Committee incurs personal liability".

The committee's enthusiasm was not to be damped by the financier's cold water and within a few days the workmen moved on to the site. It is a matter of cathedral legend that most of the bricks used in the building were actually formed and baked right on the site, there being a deposit of brick clay available.

Meanwhile a financial campaign for the necessary funds was being carried on among the friends of the church in the western parts of the huge Diocese of Toronto. The list of subscribers reads like an Upper Canadian *Who's Who*. One of the most interesting names to be found is that of Richard Guildermaster, an exiled Belgian nobleman whose full title was the Baron de Tuyll, de Seroosterkin d'Ysendoom. He was a director of the Canada Land Company and founder of the village of Bayfield on Lake Huron, built on a circular plan.

Although the list of subscribers was long, the amounts in each case were not large and the total amount of money available was far short of what was required. The rector's warden, Lawrence Lawrason, once a business partner of George J. Goodhue, personally guaranteed payment to the contractors so that the work could continue.

Sunday services continued to be held in the Mechanics' Institute. It was there, on Sunday, April 13, 1845, that the most dramatic incident in the history of the congregation of St. Paul's occurred.

It was the service of Mattins. There was a large congregation among whom was a distinguished visitor to London, the Honourable John Beverley Robinson, chief justice of the province. The justice was staying at the Robinson Hall Hotel, a frame building on the corner of Ridout and Dundas streets, just across Ridout Street from the courthouse and the

Mechanics' Institute. The hotel had been built by Peter MacGregor, London's first inhabitant, in 1832, and later sold to Dr. Hiram Davis Lee.

The officiant, the Reverend Benjamin Cronyn, gave out the Psalm for the day. It was the 68th. The rector read the first verse;

"Let God arise, let his enemies be scattered: let them also that hate him flee before him."

The people, led by the chief justice, responded:

"As smoke is driven away, so drive them away: as wax melteth before the fire, so let the wicked perish at the presence of God."

"But let the righteous be glad—" the rector began.

"FIRE!" cried a voice outside on the street. An instant's pause, and the cry was echoed by other voices.

The congregation was immobolized by fear for a moment then an uneasy movement began towards the single exit.

The auditorium was on the second floor of the Institute. A narrow staircase led to the ground floor. Panic was in the air. Had it been allowed its head, a stampede might well have resulted, with a heavy loss of life.

The rector took in the situation immediately, and in a loud voice continued the reading:

". . . let them rejoice before God: yea let them exceedingly rejoice."

Only the chief justice responded, in a clear, loud voice: "Sing unto God, sing praises to his name. . ."

On they went, rector and justice alternately reading the verses. Heartened by this display of self-control, the congregation withdrew in a quiet and orderly manner. When they were all out, Cronyn and Robinson joined them in the courthouse square.

The Robinson Hall Hotel was already doomed, and the fire was beginning to spread to adjacent buildings. At great personal risk the chief justice ran inside the blazing building and retrieved his belongings.

The local volunteer fire company was on hand with its single piece of equipment, a large reel of fire hose with a hand pump, donated to the village by George J. Goodhue.

The machine was really nothing more than a big garden sprinkler. The pump was brought up close to the building and the company began to squirt water on the blaze. Within a very few moments the intense heat drove the firemen back leaving their machine which was soon consumed by the flames. From that moment on the villagers had nothing to fight the flames with but leather fire buckets. It was soon apparent that the fire was completely out of control and all efforts at checking it were given up.

Meanwhile Cronyn, as chaplain for the garrison, had enlisted the services of some of the British Army units. Under his direction a squad of men from the Royal Artillery barracks were kept busy all day removing furniture and personal belongings from doomed buildings and piling it in the open street, where it was guarded from looters by the men of the 2nd Royal Regiment of Foot.

So rapidly and fiercely did the flames spread that more than one pile of furniture was gobbled up by the flames as soon as it had been removed to a place of apparent safety.

By mid-afternoon the entire village seemed doomed. Virtually every building south of Dundas Street was on fire and the northern half of the town was being threatened by windborne blazing timbers. Fortunately the wind came around to the north thus confining the ravages of the fire to the block in which it began and the neighbouring blocks to the south.

By nightfall the main business section of London consisted of great piles of ashes. Everything within the district bounded by Ridout, Dundas and Talbot streets and the south branch of the Thames River had been destroyed. Some 300 stores, houses, churches, banks, hotels and other buildings were swept away.

The following day the sufferers from the fire had good cause to thank Benjamin Cronyn for obtaining the services of the infantrymen. One account says that a great number of would-be "plunderers" swarmed to the site from other parts of the village and the surrounding territory, hoping for a looter's field day among the ruins, but were held at bay by the fixed bayonets of the redcoats.

Apparently the intending looters were not the only people hoping to benefit from the fire. A few Londoners endeavoured to raise funds for themselves in Toronto, representing themselves as principal sufferers in the disaster. Some were unwise enough to approach Bishop Strachan. He at once wrote to Benjamin Cronyn suggesting that he call a public meeting of "the best-known and respectable of your inhabitants" to set up a proper campaign for funds.

The proposal was swiftly acted upon and soon donations were pouring into the stricken community from cities and towns all over Canada, from the United States and Great Britain, for the story of the fire had received wide-spread publicity.

Estimates of the damage caused by London's "Great Fire" ranged as high as £300,000. No final accounting of the relief fund has been found but by the summer of 1845 it had exceeded £100,000.

The village board of police, determined there should be no repetition of the tragedy, immediately passed a by-law prohibiting the erection of any more frame buildings within the village limits

In spite of the active and heroic role played by the rector of St. Paul's in the London disaster, only one reference to the fire can be found in the cathedral records. This is in the Preacher's Book under date of April 13, 1845, where the notation occurs: "No collection—Great Fire."

Of much greater interest to the meeting of the vestry held on July 2 was the crowded state of the churchyard. From the time the first church was opened in 1834 the grounds surrounding St. Paul's had served the community as a general Protestant burial ground. Roman Catholics were interred across the street, in the grounds of St. Mary's Church, Maple and Richmond streets. The Roman Catholic church was opened in the same year at St. Paul's and its churchyard extended southward, taking in the property presently occupied by the Grand Theatre, home of the famous London Little Theatre.

By 1845 St. Paul's churchyard was proving inadequate to the needs of a growing community. The vestry accordingly agreed that, beginning on September 1, 1845, "none but members of the Church of England will be interred in the said Burial ground." A committee was named to look into the matter of beautifying the grounds and also to make inquiries "respecting the purchase of a site for a Cemetery convenient to the Town of London."

The work of this committee led St. Paul's into the cemetery business and the eventual establishment of Woodland Cemetery.

By the first of the new year St. Paul's was rapidly nearing completion. The official opening took place on Ash Wednesday, February 25, 1846, just two years to the day after the burning of the first church.

The event was well and thoroughly publicized in advance in the columns of *The London Times* whose editor and publisher, Captain Joseph Cowley, formerly an officer of the Household Guards in the reign of King George IV, was a member of St. Paul's congregation. In the issue of February 20 *The Times* gave a run-down of the events planned for the day, ending with an evening concert of which the newspaper said:

. . . as the proceeds are intended to create a fund for the purchase of an organ to celebrate the praises of the Great Jehovah, we trust no secular or sectional views will prevent the attendance of our friends.

On the day itself the church was jammed long before eleven o'clock, the hour appointed for the service to begin. The pews, intended to seat one thousand persons, proved inadequate to accommodate the numbers who sought admission. It was estimated that one thousand four hundred people were packed inside the walls while several hundred others were unable to get in.

The prayers were read by the Reverend Charles C. Brough, rector of Cronyn's old London Township parish of St. John's, and the lessons by the Reverend Francis Evans. Assisting at the Eurcharist were the Reverends Henry Revell, Thomas B. Read, Richard Flood, Mark Burnham, H. C. Cooper, James Mockridge, John Gunne, F. Sandys and the Reverend Mr. Hobson.

The rector delivered an "eloquent and appropriate" sermon in which a decided emphasis was placed upon the financial aspects of the structure. According to *The Times* he "urged the obligations Christians are under to give of their means to erect suitable temples dedicated to their worship of God; and as the design is promotion of his honour and the highest interests of man, so in general appearance, style and degree of embellishment, they should surpass rather than fall below the standard of other public edifices; and surely it is unbecoming to erect them on that meagre and mere utilitarian principle which looks for nothing more in a church than the enclosing of a given space at the lowest possible cost."

A church did not have to fall on the congregation; they took the hint. The crowded state of the building somewhat impeded the taking of the collection, but £45 was realized.

The Times' account of the opening ends with a richly opulent if not fruity, paean to the builders—the congregation of St. Paul's:

Substantial in its materials, correct in design and architecture embellished suitably to its style and character, and yet neither profuse nor extravagant in its ornaments, the present new church reflects much praise upon the spirit and Christian liberality of the churchmen of London; may it stand long uninjured by time and unscathed by casualties, to be a house of prayer, and a place of spiritual blessings to generations yet unborn.

CHAPTER SEVEN

PROSPERITY

Let there be an abundance of grain in the land, even upon the
top of the mountains.
Let its fruit wave like Lebanon, and let men flourish out of the
city like grass upon the earth.

Psalm 72: 16-17

The new St. Paul's on its completion in 1846 was one of the
most imposing church buildings in the province. Its one-
hundred-and-fourteen-foot tower crowned by four slender,
graceful pinnacles dominated the skyline of the village. The
height of the tower is today masked by the long line of the
cathedral roof.

This great tower with its four-to-six-foot-thick walls was
obviously made, as the vestry directed, for "a peal of bells."
A chime of six bells, manufactured by Mears, of London,
England, arrived at Port Stanley in 1851 and was moved from
there to London by ox-drawn wagons. They cost £500 and
were the first such bells to be brought into the province.

Externally the church was complete but it was some years
before all the interior arrangements had been finished—and
paid for. The contract for building an organ with twenty-four
stops was awarded to F. Limprecht by the vestry in April,
1850, "the cost not to exceed £300." The actual cost of the
organ, installed, proved to be £453 15s.

The heating of the church was performed by a hot air
furnace which did not always function. The evening service
of January 29, 1854, had to be stopped "owing to cold weather
and no heating apparatus." Shortly thereafter the vestry
authorized the purchase of "two of Tiffany's Patent hot air
Furnaces" for £90. The Tiffany in question was not the New
York jeweller but a local inventor of some international fame.

In spite of budget problems the church kept right up to the minute in its interior appointments. In April, 1855, the church was one of the first public buildings to be fitted for gas lighting. Previously the church had been lighted by sperm candles and oil lamps. The church journal for 1850 records the purchase of sixteen gallons of oil at a total cost of £6 and £2 worth of candles. The same statement reveals that wood was the fuel that powered the balky "hot air apparatus"— twenty cords of it at a time at approximately fifty cents a cord.

The church accounts for this same period also throw light on an exterior feature of St. Paul's, long since forgotten even by its oldest parishioners. For some years after it was opened the church had a south entrance facing on what was then known as North Street—the present Queens Avenue. A curved driveway led through ornamental gates up to a carriage platform at the south entrance so that what one contemporary writer unkindly called the "codfish aristocracy" could enter the church in inclement weather without setting foot to the ground. A short walk in the shadowy interior would bring the elite to their private pews—boxed in to protect them from the vulgar gaze, fitted with doors, locks and keys. For this privilege they paid well. Their pew rents financed the free pews "for the poor and strangers" which the rector insisted be supplied in good number. In the English manner pews at one time were sold, not rented.

In spite of the many structural changes made in the building since 1846 the church is readily identified, even in the earliest woodcuts, with the present cathedral. Comparing the first illustration of it—which appeared in Smith's *Gazetteer* in 1846—with the present building, it is seen that the church has swollen enormously to the east by the addition of transepts and chancel. The side entrance has disappeared entirely. The front of the building has changed hardly at all. The great tower stands as it has always stood, topped by its four delicate pinnacles. The early pictures show these pinnacles repeated by others on top of the buttresses along both sides of the church. The tracery they presented against the sky was most

pleasing. Unfortunately a later vestry ordered them removed
claiming they presented certain dangers to passersby in strong
winds.

The faces that look down on the passerby from every
vantage point are also unchanged. Kings, queens and mon-
strous creatures to which no human womb ever gave birth,
stare blindly out on the twentieth century, their faces chipped
and weathered by the storms and frosts of 118 years. No one
has left us any record of what these faces represent. A contemporary newspaper, *The London* (Canada) *Times,* in its
issue for 1846, devoted a whole column to a description of
the church but referred to the images only in passing. The
writer of the article—probably Dr. John Salter, surgeon, drug-
gist, former Royal Navy officer and publisher of *The London
Times*—showed a familiar knowledge of church architecture.
He was particularly fond of the tower of St. Paul's, it would
seem:

The style adopted is that which prevailed throughout the greater
part of the fourteenth century... The church consists of one large
nave, a receding chancel, a tower about three-fourths engaged, a
porch in the middle of the south side, and a small vestry on the
north side of the chancel; its total external length being 131 feet
and its width 66 feet; the Tower is 114 feet in height... The large
and lofty arched west entrance, from its depth, the door itself
being set far back, constitutes a prominent feature; above this is
a small window with a triangular crocketed canopy with finial
and corbels all executed in stone, and above this a circular aperture
for a clock. At the belfry story the tower assumes a different character; the buttresses which are diagonal and of great projection at
the base, diminish in three stages to this story when they continue
upwards in the form of octagonal turrets, detached from the tower
till connected with it half way up the story by a small piece of
masonry, where they are terminated by pointed octagonal caps
and finials. The belfry windows are large, with three lights with
flowing tracery, and the wall of this story is indented with narrow
sunk pannels terminating under the cornice with pointed arched
heads. The cornice is bold and effective, having shields at the
corners with date, and heads at intervals. The parapet is very
lofty, and the four corner pinnacles are remarkably tall with taper-
ing caps enriched with crockets and finials. Nowithstanding its
massive proportions, by the combination of the above particulars,
the architect has succeeded in giving to the upper part of the
tower that light and spiry character essential to the style.

The writer was unable to restrain the natural pride of the pioneer in seeing his adopted community's swift progress as evidence by the building of so large a church:

The erection of such a church in this part of the province is a marked step and feature in that curious and interesting, but to us familiar process by which a Country passes from the savage wildness of nature to that state of population, health and intelligence, in which the finest comforts of civilization are enjoyed in companionship with the blessings of religious ordinances and instruction.

The village which the leering gargoyles of St. Paul's now surveyed was booming and prosperous, with bright prospects for the future. The legal steps necessary for its incorporation as a town had been taken. The Act of Incorporation became law on January 1, 1848.

Even more importantly to the town's future, a railway company—the Great Western Railway—largely financed by British capital, was surveying a line between Hamilton and Windsor, passing through London. In 1847 a sod-turning ceremony for the London railway station was presided over by Lieutenant-Colonel Thomas Talbot, patriarch of the London District.

Even as the sod was being turned the immigrant fleets were putting out from the harbours of the British Isles. Like 1832, the year 1847 was a year of massive migration from the slums and the depressed farming areas of England, Ireland and Scotland. As in 1832, the immigrants brought disease with them. This time it was not cholera, but "ship's fever" (typhus). Of the ninety-eight thousand who set sail from United Kingdom ports that year, twenty thousand died on the voyage and five thousand more at the Grosse Isle quarantine station in the St. Lawrence River. An unknown number of others died in the pest houses that marked their westward route as far as the American border at Windsor.

By the first of June it was apparent that an unprecedented number of newcomers would be arriving, particularly from Ireland where the potato famine was causing terrible suffering.

On the 8th the provincial government ordered all municipalities to provide immigrant sheds for the well and hospitals for the sick.

London's Board of Police, presided over coincidentially that year by a physician (Dr. H. D. Lee), commandeered one of the village's two market houses for an immigrant shed and hastily erected near it a pest house twenty by forty feet. A second hospital of the same size was subsequently built as well as a third building for cooking and washing.

By the end of June the fever was raging among the destitute Irish at the sheds. By the end of the following month every doctor in London had been pressed into service and inspectors were examining every vehicle entering the town.

Dr. Hiram Davis Lee was chief physician. Daniel Brown and Ann Peel were the nurses. These three came into the most direct contact with the victims of the fever and by the end of October all three were dead and had been buried by the Reverend Benjamin Cronyn.

The doctor survived the longest and almost outlasted the epidemic. It was late in October, with the disease already diminishing, when he paid his last call at the hospital. It was said he spent three hours there "paying particular attention to a case whom he was very anxious to save . . . he was seen to turn aside with irresistible loathing." He died on October 29.

At the end of the first week of November the hospital was officially closed, although some patients were still being treated there. To collect food for those left in the pest house a cart, showing a placard and ringing a bell, daily paraded through the streets.

It is unfortunate that London has never erected a memorial to Dr. Lee who in happier times had been Cronyn's first host in London. A physician, and son, grandson and great-grandson of physicians, father of London's first home-grown professional actor (Graves Simcoe Lee) and the only chief magistrate of the city to die what must be considered a martyr's death, he deserves at least as much attention from his community as its first millionaire.

Since only two months of Lee's terms remained to be served at his death, no one was named president of the village

Board of Police in his stead, the chairmanship being rotated among the surviving members. In January, the new town had its first election, at which Simeon Morrill, a mattress-bearded Methodist meat-packer, was the successful candidate for the mayoralty.

The new town consisted of four wards, each named for a patron saint of the British Isles—St. George's, St. Patrick's, St. Andrew's and St. David's. Of the eight aldermen elected, two were Anglicans and members of St. Paul's Church.

The influence of the Church of England in London the Lesser was definitely on the wane.

This fact however seems to have had no real effect upon the enthusiasm and drive of the congregation of St. Paul's. The late 1840's was a period of rapid expansion for the church. In addition to completing the physical fitting of St. Paul's, the vestry pressed on with other developments. A Sunday school was established in the church in 1847 at an initial cost of £8 7s. 3d., of which the greater part was for books.

Attendance at services was large, even by today's standards, with six hundred persons being quite normal at Mattins. Until 1847 there was no evening service on Sundays—Evensong did not become an institution at St. Paul's until January 3rd of that year.

A less attractive institution at St. Paul's was the mortgage. The church was opened with a debt of £4,100. The churchwardens knew that it was no use applying to the local banks for assistance. The London banks were not in the business of loaning money to such impractical organizations as churches —or municipal councils. Early in 1848 a loan was refused the corporation of the newly-formed Town of London on grounds of insufficient security!

These four impregnable institutions—the Bank of Montreal, the Bank of Upper Canada, the Gore Bank and the Commercial Bank—were located in a row of buildings which still stands in a single block on downtown Ridout Street, a sort of miniature Wall Street. The managers, one and all, viewed with invincible suspicion any application for a loan. Not that they individually were formidable persons; it was the policy of their institutions that dictated such extreme caution.

Nor did it help the church that three of the four managers were members of St. Paul's congregation and two of them—William W. Street of the Gore Bank and Charles Monsarrat of the Commercial Bank—were churchwardens in 1847-48. Monsarrat, who came to London from the West Indies, was a great uncle of Nicholas Monsarrat, talented author of *The Cruel Sea*.

The third Anglican bank manager, James Hamilton, was responsible for preserving for posterity a record of the physical appearance of pioneer London through his many paintings of the local scene. He was a Sunday painter who while still a junior in the Toronto branch of the Bank of Upper Canada in the early 1830's exhibited at a show there with Paul Kane, being considered by Upper Canadian critics as Kane's peer. Hamilton formed a strong attachment for London and when the Bank of Upper Canada closed its doors in 1865 he bought the bank building on Ridout Street and made it his home until his death in the 1890's. In the early years of his tenure as manager he pastured a cow on the river flats behind the bank building—an indication of the primitive nature of the community at that time.

The banks being unwilling to advance the money to pay the contractors and furnishers of the new church, a former churchwarden and long-time stalwart of St. Paul's, Lawrence Lawrason, raised the funds by mortgaging his own property and by sundry notes on the banks. However, although Lawrason was one of the town's most successful businessmen the banks were unwilling to extend even to him any long term credit arrangement.

A special meeting of the vestry was held on May 29, 1848, to attempt a solution to the problem. The solution came not from the financiers and bankers but from the shrewd rector himself. It had become evident, the rector said, in his report to the vestry, "that some extraordinary means must be adopted to free the church from debt, otherwise those disinterested and zealous members of the congregation who have made themselves personally responsible for such large sums will be deeply injured."

London, Canada West, 1840   *St. Paul's Cathedral and Deanery, 1870*

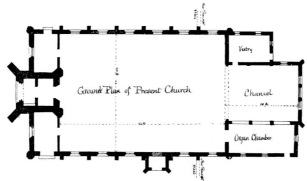

St. Paul's Cathedral Ground Plan

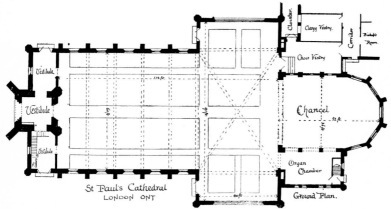

St. Paul's Cathedral *showing new Transepts and Chancel*

St. Paul's Cathedral and Synod Buildings. Perspective View

The Right Reverend
Benjamin Cronyn

The Right Reverend
Isaac Hellmuth

Cronyn's proposal was complicated as, it must be confessed, were most of his financial dealings and was based on the constantly increasing value of lands held by the church. With the permission of the Lord Bishop of Toronto he proposed selling a portion of the extensive glebe lands on what was then the eastern boundary of the town, applying a portion of the sale price to the purchase of equivalent acreage elsewhere at a lower cost and using the profit to reduce the debt of St. Paul's.

The bishop was understandably confused but granted his consent. The rector had accurately judged the condition of the real estate market. In November he reported to his superior:

In the month of July last the sale of Lot 13 (part of the glebe land) took place, and after deducting expenses, it produced £6,560. Of this one-fifth, the first instalment, has been paid, and applied to the liquidation of the debt, and as the annual payments come in the debt on the Church amounting to £3,100 will be paid, and the price of the lands purchased in exchange will also be paid.

Lot 13 consisted of one hundred and seventy-five acres within the area bounded by Dundas, Colborne and Adelaide streets and the south branch of the Thames River. The sum realized for it, the equivalent of $26,240 at the rate of exchange then current, dramatically illustrates the rapid growth of the community. Only twenty-eight years before a comparably-sized lot in the same general area had been traded by the holder of the Crown patent for a spavined ox—and the seller thought he had got the best of the bargain.

With the financial affairs of the church on a firmer footing the tenor of life in the congregation settled down to a less hectic but no less colourful rhythm. The crowded state of the churchyard and the necessity for establishing a new cemetery removed from the business area was the next crisis to overcome. Once again the rector had the solution. In 1846 he had bought a sixteen-acre lot on Dundas Street East from a former London resident. The purchase was made with Cronyn's usual acumen. By 1849 the value of the lot had increased sixfold. The location was ideal for cemetery purposes. He sold it to the church for what he had paid for it, a generosity that increased the coffers of St. Paul's quite substantially when it was sold for building lots many years later. The new cemetery was opened in the fall of 1849. By a tragic circumstance the first burial in it was that of the rector's eldest son and firstborn, Thomas Cronyn. Tom, who was born in Ireland in 1828, was at the time of his death a student at King's College (later to become the University of Toronto). A tablet to his memory was erected in the church by his fellow students and is today to be found in the north transept of the Cathedral.

Most of the bodies and gravestones were moved from the crowded churchyard to the new cemetery. One by one the ox-carts and the horse-drawn wagons transported the mouldering remains of many of London's colourful pioneers to a second resting-place. There was Dr. Archibald Chisholm, early physician of St. Thomas and London, whom Edward Boswell had buried in 1830, and there was the teen-aged girl whose memorial stone, erected by her sorrowing parents, declared that she had been "murdered by the doctors," and the four children of James Spearman, a blacksmith, who died in January, 1848, "by poison, but in what way or by whom administered is not known" according to a jury verdict.

Some remained behind—the poor whose unmarked graves were forgotten and a few respected pioneers whose survivors chose to leave them beside the church they loved. Among the latter were the old United Empire Loyalist, Lawrence Lawrason, father of the churchwarden, and an early London teacher who according to family tradition was buried under the southwest corner of the present church. The latter burial evokes memories of ancient church traditions based on even earlier, pagan sacrifices.

The old burial register of St. Paul's tells many stories to one who knows the names reported in these curt statistics. The records of the year 1850, for instance, list among many others the names of three robust pioneers of the town. Edward Matthews, at 48 an apparently successful contractor and real estate speculator, shut himself in his office at the corner of

Dundas and Richmond streets on June 22 and put a bullet
in his head, thereby ruining his lodge's plans for its semi-
annual St. John's Day celebration. A Masonic funeral was
held instead on June 24.

A little over two weeks later, on July 11, a funeral was
held for the father of London's master municipal politician,
Frank Cornish. The son's later notoriety has overshadowed
the father's equally idiosyncratic career. William King
Cornish was born in England in 1799 where he became a
solicitor. Emigrating to Upper Canada he found he could not
practise law until he had been a resident for five years. He
promptly turned to the profession of medicine, studying with
Dr. Charles Duncombe of Burford, later one of the leaders
of the Rebellion of 1837. For the balance of his relatively
brief career Cornish alternated the practice of law and
medicine, sandwiching in stints as jail physician, overseer of
highways, surveyor, coroner and clerk of the village board of
police. He had a reputation as a practical joker and rabid
Orangeman. The first is said to have cost him his lawyer's
gown and the latter credits him with having set fire to the
first log Roman Catholic Church across the street from St.
Paul's. The first story may be true, the second most certainly
not—unless the act of arson was committed posthumously.
The church burned down more than a year after Cornish's
death.

The third burial was of one William Tweedy. He died
on July 22, 1850. The following yarn is recorded in the
History of the County of Middlesex (1889):

It is related . . . that in a fight in London Township . . . a family
of Sanborns attacked a Waterloo soldier named William Tweedy,
and in the scuffle one of the Sanborns bit off the whole of his
under lip. He wrapped the piece in paper and went to Dr.
Duncombe . . . The Doctor caught a rooster, cut out of its breast
a piece to correspond with that taken out of Tweedy's lip and
stitched it in, and with the exception of no beard growing there
and a little stiffness and swelling, it appeared as good as the
original lip; but did not prove so useful, as Tweedy never afterwards could play the fife.

It is no use looking in the medical journals for a record of
this remarkable piece of plastic surgery nor is there any hope

now of discovering the late Mr. Tweedy's reaction to southern fried chicken.

Colourful as Mr. Tweedy's career seems to have been, it could not compare with that of the communicant of St. Paul's who became mayor of London in January, 1849.

Thomas C. Dixon had been a resident of London and a member of the congregation of St. Paul's for some years. He was a hatter by trade and a politician by avocation. His year's term as mayor was one of the wildest in Canadian municipal history.

At one of the first meetings of the town council for 1849 a motion was passed by his fellow-councillors over his strenuous objections. He stormed out of the council chambers. At the next succeeding meeting he refused to sign the minutes, declaring that business conducted in his absence was not legal. The feud between mayor and council continued throughout the year, resulting in a split administration and great confusion to the taxpayers.

This was the year of the Rebellion Losses Bill brought in under the aegis of Lord Elgin, one of Canada's greatest governors-general, to compensate residents of Lower Canada whose property had been destroyed during the Rebellion of 1837. The bill was bitterly contested by the Tories resulting finally in riots in both provinces, culminating with the burning of the Parliament Buildings in Montreal on April 25, 1849.

Mayor Dixon was the vociferous leader of the extreme Tory faction in London. When an effigy of Lord Elgin was publicly burned in the London marketplace on March 1 the town council demanded that action be taken against the perpetrators of the outrage. The mayor turned a totally deaf ear to the request—probably for obvious reasons.

In the following October the governor-general paid a short visit to London. The city council, over the mayor's objections, erected arches of greenery at all the principal intersections through which the vice-regal party would pass. On the morning of October 3 Dixon called a council of war at the Orange Hall where he passed out instructions and axes. Within an hour the Tory Orangemen had levelled every arch in town.

Putting on his other face, the mayor and three fellow-conspirators then rode out the Hamilton Road to meet the governor-general and to warn him with great gravity that it would be unsafe for him to visit London. Elgin is reported to have received the news in silence. He then continued into London where, contrary to the warning, he was greeted by cheering jubilant thousands.

The mayor's minority demonstration was not yet concluded however. At the Robinson Hall Hotel, across from the courthouse, the governor-general and some of the members of the reception committee addressed the crowd of more than ten thousand from an upper balcony. An address of welcome was delivered by Murray Anderson on behalf of the council. While Elgin was preparing to answer, violence broke out. According to the newspaper reports, this is what happened:

A brutal attack was made on a young man who was peaceably standing in front of the balcony, who was struck on the head by some ruffians. Immediately a rally was made by his friends and the scoundrels were beaten off. A pistol was then fired by some madman who had his skull fractured for his pains and was instantly borne off to gaol.

Relative peace was restored following this incident and the addresses continued. The troublemakers concentrated on the earl's replies to the speeches of welcome. On one occasion while Elgin was talking a group of Orangemen burst out with a chorus of yells, hisses and groans. A group of Irish armed with shillelaghs promptly hammered the demonstrators over the heads, effectively silencing them.

The self-appointed policemen were unable to silence the mayor, however. Throughout the rest of the proceedings, whenever the crowd cheered the words of the governor-general, the mayor responded with a loud, discordant groan.

At last the affair was over and the thirsty ten thousand dispersed to London's twenty-five taverns and one temperance hotel.

The town council met three days later and moved a vote of censure against Mayor Dixon. The mayor refused to put the motion and adjourned the council. The council waited until he had left, resumed the meeting and passed the motion.

The rest of the Mad Hatter's story is simply told, but is none the less extraordinary for that. He contested a provincial election against the redoubtable "Honest John" Wilson of duelling fame and lost. Shortly afterwards, pressed heavily by his creditors, he left London and removed to Hamilton. There he became a member of city council and deserted the Anglican Church to become a Mormon. He left Canada for Utah in 1854. No one would have objected to his leaving Hamilton, had he not taken with him, so it is said, the wives of five of his fellow-councillors to share his polygamous bliss. He died of the yellow fever in the 1870's in Fort Worth, Texas—sans wives, sans office.

Some of the colour went out of the life of London after the departure of Thomas C. Dixon but it was rapidly replenished from other sources.

The near-completion of the Great Western Railway un-leashed a land boom of Florida-like proportions. Over-night everyone became a real-estate speculator and an authority on land values.

Before the rails actually reached London—on December 15, 1853—the city was in the grip of as wild a real-estate boom as ever afflicted any area on the continent. Property along the right of way of the Great Western Railway suddenly assumed fantastic values. As in the city, so in the surrounding country. Property, not on the railway but in areas where it might reasonably be expected that feeder lines would be constructed later, also rose incredibly in market value. It was a rich field for the speculator. Property changed hands with dizzy speed and frequency. Fortunes were made over-night—on paper. In very few cases was the full amount of the purchase price laid on the line. An instance is recorded in the files of *The London Free Press* where one lot of land actually changed hands several times in the course of a single day—and no cash involved. It was margin buying on a scale equalled only once since in this area—in the hectic days preceding the stock market collapse of 1929. The fever reached its most insane manifestation in London. Real-estate promoters commissioned the survey of suburban building lots as far west as the village of Komoka, fourteen miles from the

westernmost limits of the town. Still other promoters laid out
suburbs five miles to the north, at Arva; ten miles to the east,
at Dorchester; and nearly to St. Thomas on the south.

If their dreams had materialized it would have required a
population larger than modern Detroit adequately to people
the physical framework of the new London. Their pre-
dictions were a long way out. Today, a century later, the
total population of the metropolitan area is only a little over
one hundred and seventy thousand—and Komoka is still fourteen miles away. As an example of the inflated values placed
on London real estate in the years between 1851 and 1857,
it will suffice to cite the case of the London businessman who
bought a building lot on the eastern fringe of the present
downtown shopping district during the boom. Unlike most
of his fellow speculators, he paid cash. For the ensuing fifty
years he paid city taxes on the lot and the building he had
erected on it. Finally, in 1905, he sold the lot and the building. He got what was then considered a good price—it lacked
a dollar of what he had paid for the lot alone a half century
before.

The cost of living spiralled upward with the cost of land.
Between 1849 and 1856 prices of foodstuffs on the London
market rose from one hundred to three hundred per cent. It
was inflation of the worst kind and disaster was its inevitable
consequence.

For a few short years however, prosperity and optimism
reigned jointly in London. The population passed 10,000
and continued to climb to a peak of 16,000 in the decade of
the 1850's. Application was made to the legislature for
London's incorporation as a city. The act became law on
January 1, 1855.

As the city grew so did the congregation of St. Paul's. The
outbreak of the Crimean War in 1853 led to the recall of the
British regiments stationed in London but their departure had
little effect on the numbers taking communion at the hands
of Parson Cronyn. "The large square pew previously reserved
for the officers of the Army" was made ready for civilian
occupancy. There was a waiting list.

It soon became apparent that the rector must have an assistant to share the burdens of the office. For a time this service was provided voluntarily by the Reverend Benjamin Bayly, principal of the London Grammar School and a member of the vestry of St. Paul's. There is no record of any payment to Mr. Bayly, but the following motion, passed at a meeting of the vestry on November 22, 1850, at which the principal was present, is indication that some kind of arrangement existed:

That the Churchwardens shall provide one or more pews at their discretion to afford accommodation to the families of any Clergymen who may be residing temporarily or permanently in London, and who may occasionally assist the Incumbent in the Services of the Church.

Two years passed before any formal arrangements for an assistant were completed. At a vestry meeting in October, 1852, Cronyn drew attention to the impending ordination of five young deacons by the Bishop of Toronto and expressed the opinion that one of these might be made available to the London church if the congregation would pledge the sum of £120 as his first year's stipend. He was prepared to provide one-half of this amount out of his own stipend, feeling the necessity of an assistant "owing to his strength not being equal to what it had been." The vestry accepted the rector's offer, the Bishop was willing and the Reverend Henry Hayward, aged thirty-one, preached his first sermon in St. Paul's at Evensong on Sunday, October 24, 1852. The collection was 11s. 3d.

The three and a half years during which the young curate served his first church (his service apparently terminated in mid-April, 1856) were exciting ones for the community. On a damp miserable evening in December, 1853, the first scheduled train on the Great Western Railway snorted into the London station after a six-hour run from Hamilton. If the land boom had been wild before, it now became quite mad.

The city and its principal church expanded explosively. Newcomers flocked into London from every point of the compass. The railway facilitated the flow of immigrants into the area. By the first of June, 1854, it was known that, as usual, they were bringing epidemic disease with them—Asiatic cholera, the most dreaded killer of them all. On June 3 Henry Hayward officiated at the burial, in St. Paul's Cemetery, of William D. Worthington, a 23-year-old railway conductor, and six Norwegian immigrants, "ages unknown." Between that date and October 25 there there 196 interments, compared with 94 in the previous year. By order of the city council, 68 victims of the pestilence were buried at night, with no clergyman officiating.

The late Dr. Edwin Seaborn in his *March of Medicine in Western Ontario* (1944) told how Henry Griffith, the Irish gravedigger, would receive the bodies of victims dumped over the cemetery wall from ox-carts, drag them to the open grave and shovel earth over them by the light of wicks stuck in a pan of grease placed on a convenient stump. The night burials were enforced by the council because of the extremely contagious nature of the disease. Contact with the bodies had no effect on Mr. Griffith. He died in 1894, aged 108, as noted in the records of St. Matthew's Anglican Church. According to close friends, his age at death was actually 118.

Most of the poorer cholera sufferers were treated in a rough wooden hospital thrown up by the city on the Hamilton road, as far as possible from the centre of the city's business and residential life.

Disease was not the only problem faced by the city fathers. Boom times, forcing a savage increase in the cost of living, created a new kind of poverty. Common labourers, previously able to maintain a precarious if sub-standard level of existence, now found themselves totally defeated by the price of foodstuffs on the London market and in grave and immediate danger of actually starving to death in the midst of plenty.

In this plight the London city council established a formal relief department, the first in London's history. A few months later while Western Ontario wheat was fetching the astonishing price of $2.64 per bushel on the London market, St. Paul's Church established the "City of London Mission" under the direction of the new assistant curate, the Reverend H. H. O'Neil, in an attempt to feed the city's poor. Thus, in one of those peculiar developments which give rise to the popular belief that "history repeats itself," there was foreshadowed an action taken by St. Paul's congregation one hundred and eight years later. (See Chapter Fifteen.)

The sufferings of the poor were of little concern to the land speculators totting up their paper profits or to the prosperous patriot worried by British reverses in the Crimean War with Russia. The incorporation of London as a city and the election of Murray Anderson, prominent local industrialist and United Empire Loyalist, as mayor loomed less large than the heroic tale of the Battle of Alma in which many officers and men of the Royal Welch Fusiliers, formerly stationed in London, gallantly fell.

Meanwhile the life of the community was being deeply enriched and variegated by the arrival of hundreds of refugee Negro slaves from the United States via the "Underground Railway." Many of the new arrivals were brought into the area by John Brown, the Kansas abolitionist whose raid on Harper's Ferry, Virginia, was one of the signposts pointing the way to the outbreak of the American Civil War.

A problem facing these refugees was solved by the action of the Church of England, to its everlasting credit. Negro parents anxious to obtain education for their children were unable to enter them in the common schools. It may come as a surprise to those natives of Ontario accustomed to viewing the racial bitterness south of the border with the detached piety of the Pharisee who thanked God he was not as other men, to learn that the public schools of the province were closed to black-skinned pupils until 1859. This, in spite of the fact that the Legislative Assembly of Upper Canada had abolished slavery as one of its first official acts in 1792, thereby earning itself the commendation of the merciful everywhere and establishing the province as a haven of the oppressed and enslaved. Demands for segregation in London continued after the desegregation order was issued in 1859, being bolstered by newspaper editorials as discriminatory as those of any back-country Georgia weekly today.

In this situation, the Colonial Church and School Society of the Church of England stepped in to fill the need. The

Reverend Isaac Hellmuth, of whom much more will be told in these pages, was appointed general secretary for North America. Under his direction missions and schools for the benefit of fugitive slaves were established in connection with Trinity and St. George's churches in Montreal. The biggest establishment in the Society's work however was that opened first in an empty building in the former military barracks in London, and later in the Sunday school building on the grounds of St. Paul's Church.

The Reverend Martin Dillon, formerly an officer in Her Majesty's 89th Regiment when stationed in the Leeward Islands, British West Indies, was appointed to the charge of the London mission and school. As the Preacher's Book of the Cathedral shows, he also frequently assisted the rector and his assistant in services at the church. To help him in his work, Mr. Dillon engaged the services of Sarah and Mary Ann Titre, natives of Dominica. This, he claimed in a report to the Society, was "the first instance, either in the United States or in this country, in which coloured persons have been introduced as teachers of mixed classes."

The connection of the church with the Negro problem reached its climax in 1855 when more than 700 fugitives from slavery marched from the barracks grounds to attend a service in St. Paul's Church on the occasion of the celebration of Emancipation Day (August 11, anniversary of the enactment of Britain's anti-slavery legislation in 1832).

Following the church service where Martin Dillon preached from John 13: 34—"A new commandment I give unto you, that ye love one another"—a civic luncheon was held attended by the mayor and council as well as many of London's leading citizens.

It is unfortunate that more is not known about this school, its pupils and their later success—or failure. References are disappointingly meagre. That at least it fulfilled the expectations of the general secretary for North America of the Colonial Church and School Society is seen from a report made by Dr. Isaac Hellmuth after a visit to the school in 1859:

Accompanied by Dr. Cronyn I attended my first Adult School, consisting entirely of coloured people . . . It was an interesting sight to see so many grown up men and women sitting like little children to be instructed in the first rudiments of both secular and religious knowledge.

The first decade of the new church of St. Paul's had been packed with enough excitement for a century. The congregation, with scarcely a pause in its stride, had undertaken the crushing financial burden of building and equipping a huge new church and of meeting the needs of the community for cemetery facilities, had engaged with gusto in land speculation to its great future profit, had endured a savage epidemic, taken steps for the alleviation of the suffering of the poor and co-operated with the mother church in supplying educational opportunity for refugee Negro slaves, in the face of general community apathy if not opposition.

However, nothing in this stirring record can match for sheer Christian exoticism, the picture of Isaac Hellmuth, the converted Polish Jew, himself a fugitive from religious intolerance, facing a classroom full of careworn Negroes fresh from the slave markets, shiny black faces glowing with the unaccustomed exertion of education and the sun of freedom.

Nothing even in the ecstatic apostleship of St. Paul can offer a scene to better this.

It was well that none of these participants had the gift of prophecy. For the students, the future held indifferent or contemptuous tolerance from their fellow-citizens and social confinement to "Nigger Hollow;" for their visitor, the grudging respect of lesser men, the dizzy heights of intellectual accomplishment—and heartbreak.

They would not have chosen to know their future. For them was the heat of battle, the exhilaration of the day's accomplishment. With James Graham, seventeenth-century Marquis of Montrose, they might have declared:

> He either fears his fate too much,
> Or his deserts are small,
> That dares not put it to the touch,
> To win or lose it all.

CHAPTER EIGHT

CATHEDRAL

They prayed and said, Thou, Lord, which knowest the hearts of all men, shew whether of these two thou hast chosen, that he may take part of this ministry and apostleship from which Judas by transgression fell, that he might go to his own place. And they gave forth their lots and the lot fell upon Matthias; and he was numbered with the eleven apostles.

Acts 1: 24-26

For the congregation of St. Paul's the year 1857 marked the beginning of a glamorous new career as the cathedral church of the newest Canadian diocese of the Church of England. For the cathedral's community it signaled the onslaught of a period of stress and hardship without parallel in Canadian municipal history.

Chronologically the church's triumph came first. The story of the establishment of the Diocese of Huron and the election of Dr. Benjamin Cronyn (he had been granted an honorary degree by his alma mater, Trinity College, Dublin, in 1855) as its first bishop has been told many times. The latest and one of the most thoroughly-documented accounts is to be found in the biography of Cronyn by the late Reverend Dr. A. H. Crowfoot. It will consequently be alluded to only briefly here. Actually adequately to recount the full tale of that ecclesiastical landmark would require a book by itself.

In the first place it was the first *election* of a bishop in the history of the Canadian church. All previous Canadian bishops had been named by the Crown (as English bishops still are).

In the second place the Canadian newspapers (notably *The London Free Press*) had decided in advance of the election who the two chief candidates would be, promoted a dispute between the two and opened their columns generously for the ensuing, highly-unedifying "episcopal controversy." The correspondence, which began on a reasonably genteel tone came perilously close to Billingsgate before its conclusion.

81

A compilation in book form achieved some notoriety and a small circulation.

The dispute did not require much fanning to bring it to white heat for, in the third place, Bishop Strachan of Toronto who presided at the first synod of the Diocese of Huron was known to be positively opposed to London's "favourite-son" candidate, Dr. Cronyn, and favoured the pretensions of the second candidate, Archdeacon Alexander N. Bethune, of Cobourg.

In the fourth place, the controversy involved that perennial bone of contention in the English Church—"high church versus low." The affiliation of the respective antagonists in the Cronyn-Bethune feud is best illustrated by the comment of Bishop Strachan in a letter to the SPG written in June, 1851:

Mr. Cronyn has been the focus of all the agitations against the Society's plans and me for supporting peace and order among the clergy of that western section . . . he is a low-churchman, and better fitted for a political agitator than a Bishop.

The synod took place in St. Paul's on Wednesday and Thursday, July 8/9, 1857. Contrary to the avid expectations of the newspaper press, the proceedings were dignified and solemn in the extreme. This was largely due to the precautions taken by Bishop Strachan who had been so appalled by the "odious proceedings" during the public canvassing by the two principal candidates that he had determined on a highly deliberate and slow-moving agenda for the synod. Thus little was accomplished on the first day beyond solemn services and ratifications of all delegates.

Despite the lack of fireworks at the initial session, the galleries of St. Paul's were crowded with interested spectators on Thursday morning. The clergy took their positions in the pews on the right side of the church, the lay delegates on the left.

Anticipating a demonstration in spite of his precautions, the Bishop gave a last warning to all participants and spectators prior to the actual balloting:

I trust that the proceedings will be conducted in such a manner as to show that you all, my brethren, feel the serious nature of

this great occasion. I ask that there be no manifestation of feeling, and I beg of you to pay due respect to the solemnity of the
occasion and the sacredness of this edifice in which we are
assembled.

The roll was then called and a short period of silence
observed for Divine guidance (sorely needed on this occasion).
The balloting began, first among the clergy and then the
laity. It was completed at 11:30 A.M.

Only one ballot was needed. Dr. Cronyn received twenty-
two votes from the clergy and twenty-three from the laity;
Archdeacon Bethune got twenty clergy votes and ten lay
votes. Bishop Strachan immediately declared Dr. Cronyn
elected first bishop of the Diocese of Huron.

Despite all warnings, this was too much for the Londoners
crowded into the galleries. A thunderous cheer went up.

"SILENCE!" boomed the bishop.

(Every writer who tells this story always capitalizes the
word. I see no reason why I should be different.)

This very brief outburst was the only undignified note in
the entire proceedings. Bishop Strachan had achieved a
harmonious solution to the "episcopal controversy." The
reason for his great care is plainly seen in a later comment:

It was refreshing to witness the triumph of Christian unity and
love. This threw to the winds all the arguments against the free
and honest choice of Bishops which the narrower selfishness of
many centuries had mustered up.

Although the Crown (in the person of Queen Victoria and
her advisers) had permitted the Canadian election to be held,
consecration had still to be performed in England at the hands
of the Archbishop of Canterbury. The bishop-elect sailed
soon after the synod concluded, was consecrated in the chapel
of Lambeth Palace on St. Simon and St. Jude's Day (October
28) and returned to Canada to preach his first sermon as
bishop in his cathedral church of St. Paul's on Christmas Day.

The London he returned to had changed drastically and
tragically in his absence.

The first hint of trouble had come in January, 1857. An
American newspaper reported that the British economic depression, inevitably following in the wake of the Crimean

War, had spread to this continent and that in New York City alone one hundred thousand men were unemployed. By March the local newspapers were complaining about "tight money."

The full fury of the storm was still some months off when the farmers of Western Ontario seeded their fields to wheat that spring. They were soon more concerned with the Canadian weather than with the daily reports of bank failures in the United States. The growing season started off badly, with torrential rains that continued into late May and delayed sowing operations. June was cold and gloomy. The first two weeks in July were a decided improvement (perhaps in honour of the Huron synod). Then, just as it appeared the crop would have a chance after all, a late frost struck. A farmer near Komoka rose early and went out to have a look at his crop. The stalks of the wheat were bent half over with the weight of frost-split and soggy kernels. The farmer returned to his house and blew out his brains. By September it was apparent that the crop failure was general throughout the continent. The harvest of the pitifully-reduced yield was about to begin when the rains returned. What was still standing in the fields was drowned out.

The one ray of light in the gloom was the continuing high price of grain, caused by the short supply. Once the local harvest began moving to the export markets it was felt conditions in London would improve. However the local banks, cautious as always, but doubly so in view of the general panic, refused to advance money to the London wheat merchants. *The London Free Press* editorialized on the situation:

The present monetary and commercial crisis is unquestionably the severest that has visited this continent for many years. Already many of the leading banking institutions of the chief cities of the United States . . . have succumbed or suspended. Public confidence has ceased to exist, commercial enterprises are completely checked . . . and stagnation, gloom and panic pervade the land. That we in Canada are deeply affected by this state of things in the neighbouring republic, as well as by the tightness of the money market in England, in unquestionable. The Banks, as a measure of precaution, have limited their discounts to the lowest possible figure. They do not feel themselves justified even in advancing the means to our wheat merchants to enable them to render available the produce of the last harvest. This was what our merchants and people had chiefly to depend upon; and, with the staple products of the country locked up in our granaries, our condition must be from bad to worse . . . with the channels of commerce comparatively dried up, our staple products kept out of the market, the labours of the mechanic suspended for want of capital, little or no money in the hands of the people, and a gloomy winter close upon us, we have sufficient cause for serious reflection, and for asking the question, can nothing be done to relieve us?

The panic had been somewhat late in reaching London, but when it struck, it was with a savagery unequalled elsewhere in North America. There were three good reasons why this was so. In the first place, most London businesses of the 1850's were small shoestring family affairs, less able than large, wealthy manufacturing concerns to weather financial storms. Not until the discovery of oil in Western Ontario in the 1860's did London become the centre of any large industry. The second cause was the one-crop economy of the farming area upon which London depended. As the price of wheat went, so did London's prosperity, and with the yield reduced, and as *The Free Press* stated "locked up in the granaries," the flow of foreign exchange was reduced to a trickle. The third cause was the era of wild speculation in real estate which had preceded the collapse. In this respect, *The Free Press* commented in the fall of 1857, about the time Bishop Cronyn was being consecrated at Lambeth Palace:

Almost the whole of those businessmen who attended to their legitimate occupations, letting speculation in town lots and bogus villages alone, have stood and will stand their ground.

During the next two frightful years, Londoners turned back the pages. Then, as in the early years of the city's history, the chief industry of its citizens became litigation. The debtors' courts handled the greatest volume of business and in this, as in other aspects of the depression, London established an unenviable record. From their inception the London courts had been notorious for the stringency with which they administered Canada's mediaeval debtors' laws. Under the brutal Debtors' Act, an outmoded civil law inherited from the

Mother Country, a creditor could secure the imprisonment of a man or woman for non-payment of a debt as small as forty dollars. The injustices practised under this Act were even worse than those crusaded against by Charles Dickens in England. The Canadian prisons were smaller and more crowded than their English counterparts and the treatment accorded the debtors more brutal. And nowhere in Canada were the conditions as bad as in London. A local newspaper took the stand that, were it not for the operation of this vicious law, many hard-pressed businessmen would have stuck it out until the tide turned, instead of running for the border when the shadow of the debtors' prison fell close upon them:

We unhesitatingly affirm, dispute it who may, that by far the largest proportion of the disaster that has fallen upon this place has arisen from the course complained of, and that those who practise it are the worst enemies of the city. In no other place in Canada has this mania prevailed; but to such an extent is it carried on here, that London has become a bye-word in the Province, as containing plenty of lodging room in the houses, but none in the jail.

By the end of 1859 it was only too bitterly obvious that there was no lodging room in the London jail. There came to be a general relaxation in the exercise of the law, by virtue of necessity. It is no exaggeration to say that, between September, 1857, and September, 1859, three-quarters of the small businesses of the city went under. The debtors' apartments were no longer able to take care of the waiting list. By the end of 1859 it became apparent also that the exercise of the Debtors' Act had had a marked effect upon the population figures of the city, which dropped from 16,000 in 1855 to 11,000 in 1859.

Meanwhile the suffering among the poor of the city had become intense. The city council established a soup kitchen in connection with the municipal hospital. All day long indigents lined up there to receive their dole, but when the kitchen's food quota for the day had been exhausted, there were still scores of empty bellies. Before the end of the three years of economic purgatory that closed in 1860, municipal funds had proved totally inadequate to the emergency and a public subscription list was opened for the relief of the poor.

In the heart-breaking attempts to meet this staggering challenge, the churches of the city, including St. Paul's, played an active and gallant part, as did also the various charitable and fraternal organizations. St. Paul's Cathedral operated one of the five major public soup kitchens which strove, unsuccessfully, to cope with the tide of want.

This was a particularly inauspicious setting for the work of the new diocese. Bishop Cronyn's comment in a letter to the secretary of the SPG, that on his return he had found "pecuniary matters in a very disturbed state," must be taken as a masterpiece of understatement. Nevertheless the work had to go forward and so at the beginning of January, 1858, he summoned his clergy and lay delegates to meet with him at St. Paul's. They met on the 28th of that month to transact a very necessary item of business—the establishment of a Church Society for the diocese. At this period and for many years after, the finances of the Canadian dioceses were managed by these societies, leaving the synods free to discuss all other matters.

An interesting feature of the establishment of the Huron Church Society was the transfer to it of all church property, land and buildings, including the cathedral church of St. Paul's. The Society then leased the cathedral and its lands to the rector and corporation of St. Paul's for 999 years with an option of renewal for a further 999 years at a yearly rental of one peppercorn.

It is assumed that when the synod of the Diocese of Huron absorbed the Huron Church Society it fell legal heir to all legal arrangements of the Society including the St. Paul's lease. I very much fear that the rent is seriously in arrears as I can find no record of any peppercorns changing hands for a great many years back. If the ordinary of the Diocese of Huron ever finds himself in need of seasoning for his table, he knows where to go.*

---

*The cathedral's delinquency having been brought to the attention of the diocesan authorities in the fall of 1964, payment was made to the Right Reverend George N. Luxton, Bishop of Huron, by the Very Reverend Kenneth B. Keefe, Dean of Huron, of one hundred peppercorns in a brief ceremony at the doors of the cathedral.

The arrangement as it stands in the old deed is complicated enough, but when one realizes that the president of the Church Society was also the Bishop of Huron, who was also rector of St. Paul's, the complexity of the peppercorn situation (as well as the other financial affairs of the diocese) becomes such that only an Irish Cronyn could ever keep it straight.

All the bishop's shrewdness of mind and Christian enthusiasm were needed to cope with the problems of the new diocese. Eight letters from as many different sections of Western Ontario brought to his attention the desperate need for clergy. One settler in Bruce County wrote that he had been living in the bush for three years without ever seeing a clergyman.

It was at this time that a project began to form in the bishop's mind whereby a more adequate provision might be made for the training of clergy for the western diocese. A divinity school was needed in his see city, London. The project was received with little sympathy in Toronto for it was abundantly obvious to all that any theological college established by the "low-church" Bishop of Huron would have a pronounced evangelical colouring.

Daunted not at all by the opposition of the Bishop of Toronto, Cronyn went ahead with his plans. He found a strong and eager ally in the Polish-born general secretary for North America of the Colonial Church and School Society. The Reverend Isaac Hellmuth had visited London numerous times in connection with the work of the refugee Negro school under his jurisdiction. On these occasions it is apparent that he and the bishop had had a number of fruitful conversations, the subject of which was never made public. In view of later events, it is of some significance to note that Hellmuth was given a seat on the floor of the house at Cronyn's first synod, in September, 1858.

From the private talks between these two men were to come Huron College, the theological school of the Diocese of Huron, and all the other school-building activities of the 1860's.

CHAPTER NINE

WAR

Out of the south cometh the whirlwind: and cold out of the north.
Job 37: 9

London in the 1860's was a totally different place from the boom-mad town of the Frantic Fifties. Economic disaster had stamped on its remaining citizens an indelible brand of financial scepticism which remained their chief characteristic for a century to come. The optimists and the inveterate adventurers went with the five thousand who deserted the town between 1856 and 1859. Only the pessimists and the poor were left.

This is not to say that all the colour went out of London with the passing of the great depression. The city was not yet ready to settle down into the determined conservatism that was to mark it in the dying decades of the nineteenth century. It was still a frontier town. The saloons still had swinging doors and through them passed a host of characters who had not yet hardened into types.

In fact the decade of the 1860's supplied enough excitement in London to last a generation and in the result that is what it had to do, for the decade that followed was singularly barren of incident.

The first half of the decade was marked by the advent of the American Civil War and the mayoralty of Francis Evans Cornish. It would be hard to say which event made the greatest impact on London. Chronologically, the two followed a parallel course. The Civil War and Cornish both erupted in 1861 and Cornish was finally defeated shortly before his contemporary, General Robert E. Lee.

An abbreviated biographical notice of Francis Evans Cornish appeared in Chapter Two where he entered the history of St. Paul's Cathedral by the undramatic process of being baptized in February, 1831, by the Reverend E. J. Boswell, first incumbent of St. Paul's. His birth and baptism were the last undramatic events in the life of Frank Cornish.

Francis Cornish was admitted to the Bar in 1852, in his 21st year, and appointed a Queen's Counsellor three years later, the youngest Q.C. in Canadian legal history to that date. He was already persona non grata with *The London Free Press*, largely because of his political activities and his appointment brought a stinging editorial blast. Despite the paper's opposition—or perhaps because of it—he finally succeeded in achieving aldermanic honours in 1858, representing the old seventh ward.

Three years' experience in ward politics convinced Frank that he was the people's choice and in 1861 he ran successfully for the office of mayor which he retained for four consecutive terms. The Cornish formula for electoral success was childishly simple and was made possible by the outbreak of the American Civil War.

It must be realized that the threshold of this bloody struggle was only one hundred and twenty miles from London's doorstep—the distance from this city to Detroit, Michigan. Gettysburg is only some three hundred airline miles from London's Covent Garden market. It was inevitable that the citizenry should be keenly interested in the conflict and apprehensive about its results.

Apprehension turned to naked fear when a Union vessel stopped a British ship, the *Trent*, on the high seas and seized two Confederate commissioners in the fall of 1861. The "*Trent* incident" brought Great Britain and the United States to the verge of war. While the dispute was settled without bloodshed, it gave the Northern press an excuse to revive old dreams of American supremacy over the entire continent. From that time until the war's end—and after—the theme was a recurring one in the editorial columns of the newspapers of New York, Chicago and Detroit.

While the war scare was at its height the British government dispatched ten thousand seasoned troops to the defence of British North America. Of these, two thousand were sent to London. The still-habitable portions of the old log and framed barracks were refurbished for their reception and a number of public and private buildings in the centre of the town were requisitioned as well. As the Americans continued to rattle a tentative sabre periodically throughout the decade, the Imperials remained until after Confederation.

It was the presence of the British soldiers that provided Frank Cornish the voting power needed for his political machine.

A provincial law granted the municipal franchise to all male British subjects over the age of twenty-one who could prove twenty-four hours' residence within the municipality. The British soldiers being stationed, for the most part, in barracks situated on property owned by the Imperial government were ineligible for the local vote. However, on the promise of unlimited liquid refreshment and other favours many of the rank and file were only too glad to oblige Frank Cornish by taking up residence in the city proper on a temporary basis—for, say, twenty-four hours. At the end of that time, being legally entitled to exercise their franchise, they swarmed to the polls with great enthusiasm. Being strangers in the town, they almost invariably voted for the man they knew best who, by coincidence, always happened to be Francis Evans Cornish.

It was a stirring sight, on the first day of the annual election, to see the hundreds of brave redcoats, staggering, weaving and crawling from the tented mushroom city in that section of North London known as "Tipperary Flats," thence to proceed with much chaffing, singing and fighting to the polls, there to cast their verbal votes for that fine gentleman, Mr. Cornish, the uncrowned king of London.

At the hustings also the Cornish machine functioned with a smooth efficiency. The secret ballot was then unknown and the elector had to declare his choice in a loud, clear voice to the returning officer and the clerks. During the Cornish reign, before the elector could perform this simple task, he had first to penetrate a cordon of the mayor's party policemen.

If he were a known Cornish supporter he would be greeted with cordiality, with touched caps, brotherly greetings and friendly salutes with cudgel, baton and shillelagh. Should he, however, be an avowed adherent of David Glass, perennial opponent of the mayor, his penetration of the line would be quite another matter. If he succeeded in casting his vote at all, it was accomplished at the expense of a positively Churchillian amount of blood, sweat and tears.

It was an almost fool-proof system and operated with great success for four consecutive elections. It failed on the fifth occasion ironically enough, due to the unprincipled use by his opponent of the soldiery—the militia, this time. In January, 1865, David Glass talked the city council into calling out the citizen soldiers to protect his supporters and won on the third day of voting.

The flamboyant mayor suited a community that, for the four troubled years of the Cornish reign, existed on almost a wartime basis. Towards the end of the American Civil War, when the Confederate States were making a last-ditch, hopeless stand against the overwhelming power of the Union, London was a miniature Lisbon with spies, counter-spies and counter-counter-spies rubbing elbows with Pinkerton detectives, Confederate and Union officers in mufti, southern refugees, fugitive Negroes and even a few plain London citizens. The reason for all this cloak-and-dagger activity was the ill-fated "Northwest Conspiracy"—a final mad attempt by the Confederate States of America to turn the tide of the war by harassing the Union Army from the north, from Canada. London was for a time an important link in the communications chain of the Confederate conspiracy.

From the beginning of the war many Southern refugees sought shelter in London where they were pampered by the well-to-do families, who sympathized with the Confederacy, and scorned by the common people who by and large, supported the North.

One of the first arrivals made St. Paul's Cathedral his ecclesiastical "home away from home" and subsequently involved the church in some unwelcome notoriety. He was the Reverend W. Herbert Smythe, formerly of the parish of St.

John's, Helena, Arkansas, Confederate States of America. Smythe arrived in London in the early spring of 1862 and attended the meeting of the Huron Church Society on March 13. Although his name does not appear in the official records of St. Paul's, he seems to have had some undefined connection with the church and was, in at least one instance, referred to as an assistant curate at St. Paul's.

Smythe took up residence at Strong's Hotel on Dundas Street near Richmond. With him were his two children (there is no reference anywhere to a Mrs. Smythe) and two Negroes —a young boy, unnamed, and a young woman named Elizabeth Smith (or Smythe). He termed them his servants. The Negro colony in London seems to have assumed that they were slaves.

Sometime in August, 1862, the hotel proprietor, Henry Strong, warned Smythe that "a plot was being concocted by certain parties" to abduct Elizabeth. The cleric paid no heed until the last Sunday in August when two coloured people called at the hotel and tried to induce Elizabeth to go with them. Later that afternoon he took Elizabeth and the two children to a service at St. Paul's. Trouble occurred as they were returning. He related the details before Mayor Cornish, acting as police magistrate, on August 25:

Whilst returning from church, he saw the two defendants approaching. He and his servant were leading one of the children; suspecting their intentions, he and his party crossed over the street to the other side . . . The defendants followed closely and very rudely seized hold of his servant's arm, pushing him and his child off the sidewalk. He then said to his servant that "as the dark ladies required so much room in walking, they (witness and party) should cross the street".

The "dark ladies" followed, Smythe testified, pushing the clergyman and forcing him and his party "against windows, shutters, lamp-posts and walls." Throughout this they kept urging Elizabeth to come with them, telling her that she was in a free country and threatening her with the use of force if she would not come peacefully. The party reached the safety of their hotel finally, following which Smythe laid information against the two Negro women.

Smythe informed the crowded courtroom that the boy in his charge had been "given" to him by an English lady, from whom he also got Elizabeth. It is perhaps significant that he testified he had been "given" the boy but "got" Elizabeth. However, on her own behalf Elizabeth declared that she had never been owned "by anyone but her mother." She further stated that she had been the clergyman's servant "on and off" for two years and was aware that "she was free in Canada, without (the defendants) enlightening her on that point."

One C. Davis, appearing on behalf of the defendants, said he had spoken to Elizabeth Smythe [sic] on two occasions and that in reply to his queries she had admitted that she was a slave. Then he dropped his bombshell. Rumour, he said, had it that "Elizabeth is a daughter of Mr. Smythe's brother."

It was this rumour apparently that had fanned public interest in the case. No reply was forthcoming from Mr. Smythe or anyone acting on his behalf and in the result the community's curiosity had to go unsatisfied. The proceedings wound to a close without any action being taken against the defendants. The bench warned them but imposed no fine or other penalty, "Mr. Smythe stating he had no feelings to gratify in the matter," merely wishing protection from annoyance.

The clergyman, English by birth, became something of a social lion in succeeding months, several times being called upon to address London organizations on his impressions of the war between the states and on life within a slave state.

Reading between the lines, however, it is fairly apparent that Smythe's continued presence in London, with its large Negro population—mainly refugees from the slave states—was a source of embarrassment to the church.

The matter was settled amicably before Christmas, 1862.

In November Bishop Cronyn appointed Smythe to the parish of Holy Trinity, Teeswater, in Bruce County. With that, he disappears from the history of St. Paul's.

Meanwhile, amid all the electoral excitement and rumours of war, events of more lasting importance to the Church of England and the city of London were brewing in St. Paul's rectory. This handsome building, erected by the church in

1854, was the residence of a succession of rectors until its demolition in 1955. Here the new Bishop of Huron conferred with his new assistant rector, the Reverend Isaac Hellmuth, on the best means of supplying the great need for clergy in the infant diocese.

Hellmuth, like Cronyn, was a staunch evangelical. Like Cronyn he had no wish to flood the Diocese of Huron with graduates from the "high-church" Trinity College of Toronto. The only alternative was to establish a new college. Accordingly, on October 22, 1861, Hellmuth (now Archdeacon of Huron) set sail for England "to raise funds for the establishment of a sound Evangelical College from which men may be sent forth to proclaim the Gospel of Jesus Christ in all godly simplicity and fullness."

In the midst of his herculean labours to provide an Anglican ministry for a rapidly-increasing church population throughout his diocese, Bishop Cronyn did not forget the needs of his cathedral church or his see city.

The cathedral was still experiencing severe financial difficulties arising from the construction of a large church and an equally large rectory within a period of ten years. The rectory, built during the land and wheat boom, cost more than the church—$16,004.87. A report on the cost, made by a special committee of the vestry of St. Paul's on February 28, 1862, strikes an uncomfortably familiar note to modern ears:

The cost is certainly very great but it must be kept in mind that the Rectory and the out houses were erected at a time when labour and material were extremely high.

On this occasion, as on many others, the bishop-rector came to the assistance of his favourite church. The vestry minutes record his action:

His Lordship the Bishop then addressed the Vestry expressing his great anxiety that the debt of the Church should be lowered and matters placed in a better position, and that he now held in his hand Debentures amounting to three thousand five hundred & seventy dollars & ninety cents and interest due on the same amounting to one hundred & sixty dollars & sixty-seven cents which he had now cancelled and gave as a donation to assist to lesson [sic] the Church debt.

In the motion thanking the bishop for his generosity it was also noted that the previous week his lordship had given £1,000 ($4,000) "for the same object."

The state to which the finances of the cathedral had sunk is apparent from the decision taken in September, 1861, to dispense with the services of the organist, bell ringers and pew opener. The greatest loss was that of the organist. The key-board was not vacant for long, however, owing to an extraordinary arrangement made by the churchwardens in January, 1862:

Resolved: That Mr. McMullen (Thomas F. McMullen, sexton of St. Paul's) be requested to hand to Mr. Luard the Deed of ¼ Lot in the Cemetry [sic] & funeral expenses free of charges also a receipt for his back pew-rent on consideration of Mr. Luards giving his service free, in playing the organ of St. Paul's Church.

The sequel to this peculiar arrangement is found in the minutes of the board for October 5, 1863:

It was reported that Mr. T. D. Luard who has for the past 18 months acted gratuitously as organist had resigned that duty, being about to proceed to England. It was resolved that Mrs. Raymond, a person of high respectability & an excellent organist, be appointed organist at a salary of $100 p. annum.

This pleasant and somewhat amusing little interlude had a tragic and unexpected conclusion. Young Mr. Luard did not go to England and he did require the plot in the cemetery. The story is told by a wall plaque in the south transept of the cathedral:

In memory of Rev. Thomas Davis Luard, born at Goderich, educated at King's College, London, ordained at this Cathedral Oct. 28th, 1863, died on the seventh day following, aged 26 years.

At the next meeting of the board a sum of $20 was contributed "towards the testimonial . . . to the Rev. T. D. Luard" by which presumably is meant the wall tablet. Luard's successor, Mrs. Elizabeth Raymond, wife of a pioneer London hat-maker, served the church for thirteen years.

The terms of office of the cathedral employees tended to lengthen as the city slowly settled into a more staid Victorian pattern. Thomas McMullen the sexton mentioned above, was a case in point. He served the church for twenty-one years—from 1852 to 1873. Towards the end he became somewhat irascible, as a board minute for November, 1864, indicates:

Resolved that although the annoyance caused by unruly children in and about the church is much to be regretted, yet the church-wardens forbid the use of violence on the part of the Sexton in such cases and request that if he should find expostulation insufficient, he will report any case of disturbance or improper conduct to the church-wardens.

It would appear that juvenile delinquency was not confined to the church grounds for about this same time the board was obliged to hire a special constable to patrol the cemetery grounds on Dundas Street at a fee of seventy-five cents per day.

During the early part of the decade the minutes of the board were frequently signed, in the absence of the bishop, by his efficient assistant, the Reverend John McLean, who succeeded the Reverend H. H. O'Neill in 1858. After nine years at the cathedral Mr. McLean moved on, capping a brilliant career in 1874 when he was consecrated first Bishop of Saskatchewan. He died in 1886.

Mr. McLean was succeeded as assistant by the Reverend G. H. Low, later a canon and rector of Billings' Bridge, Diocese of Ottawa. His successor was the Reverend George Mignon Innes, who was appointed to the post in 1868. He was fated to have a long and intimate connection with the cathedral.

Mr. Innes' association with St. Paul's actually dated to 1862, when he was assigned by Bishop Cronyn to the mission which, a year later, became Christ Church, London, the first of the cathedral's numerous daughter churches.

The bishop had already decided on the site of the new church—Wellington Street at Hill Street—land which he himself had donated. Meanwhile Sunday services were held at the nearby Central School. On week nights outdoor services were conducted on the church site. The *History of the County of Middlesex* (1889) tells an amusing story about one of these services:

In lieu of a better stand, the missionary used to speak from the top of an old hollow stump, with a congregation of from 60 to 100 gathered about on the grass. On the occasion in question, some mischievous boys had filled the stump with dry leaves, which, in the middle of the sermon, they contrived to set on fire. The preacher had speedily to descend from his perch and seek a cooler atmosphere.

With true Victorian hyperbole the account concludes: "Above the ashes of the old stump arose the present pulpit." What *did* arise in place of the stump was what the late Dr. A. H. Crowfoot called "one of the purest specimens of Gothic architecture to be found in the diocese." Christ Church with its soaring interior arches is just one of the 101 churches erected in the diocese during the episcopacy of its first bishop.

The same year that saw the consecration of Christ Church also marked the opening of Huron College. Archdeacon Hellmuth's "begging tour" of England had been highly successful. The money he had raised was used to buy "Rough Park," an estate in North London, to alter it for college use and to hire a staff. The inauguration ceremony was held on December 6, 1863. Normally, such an affair would have been graced by the presence of one or more high-ranking officers from the British garrison. However the London garrison had been drastically reduced in the spring as a disciplinary move following a disgraceful fist fight between Mayor Frank Cornish and the barracks commandant.

The mayor was not alone in his aversion to the military. The following year a pitched battle took place between civilians and soldiers—luckily without loss of life—over the question of a right of way along the west side of the barracks property. The soldiers actually wheeled up some field pieces in an effort to intimidate the civilians but without result—too many of the citizens were Irish. The triumphant Londoners removed the barricades placed by the Imperials and from that day to this Clarence Street has been an undisputed public right of way.

Threats by the commander in chief of the British forces in Canada to remove the garrison from London entirely were greeted with equanimity by the mayor and his friends and sympathizers but, understandably, not by the merchants whose views were expressed in *The London Free Press:*

The consequences . . . are obvious. On the removal of the troops, house rents will fall thirty or forty per cent; trade, which has been active, will diminish; the minor produce from the country, which has risen largely in price, will fall; and thus not only will the citizens of London, but the farmers in the neighbourhood, be called upon to suffer.

These fears were entertained only briefly. Worsening relations between Great Britain and the United States, irritated further by the warlike activities of the Confederate agents in Canada, led to the return of the garrison to full strength in 1864.

There were other nine-day wonders to keep the citizenry tittivated in the last full year of the war. A long series of incendiary fires which left a half dozen or more gaping holes in the city's main business section on Dundas Street began early in 1864. Forty citizens were organized in a sort of vigilance committee to aid the overworked fire department and to bring the culprit to justice but without success, despite a $200 reward. One of the city's financial guardians defaulted—he was not the first to do so, nor would he be the last. A gigantic financial row took place between the City Council and the School Board—again not the first, nor the last. The amateur actors of London put on a special three-day celebration of the tercentenary of the birth of William Shakespeare. Stratford's festival was to have been the big one, but no one was able to work up any enthusiasm there.

Other alarms and excursions uncomfortably close to home kept the citizens in a constant state of nerves. A race riot in Detroit, an attack on a Negro settlement near Oil Springs by a number of American workmen, a riot in Windsor and a battle in Lake Erie between a Union vessel and a ship bearing the Confederate flag, kept the pot boiling and the newspapers full of catastrophe.

Amid all this excitement, thirteen candidates for the ministry were prepared for ordination at Huron College and the

sexton of St. Paul's Cathedral got into difficulty with the silver
in the collection plates.

A wartime devaluation of American silver money had led
to a rather serious situation in Canada where most of the
coinage in circulation was either British or American. In
consequence Canadian banks had decided to refuse to accept
silver money. Confronted with a growing hoard of silver
from the Sunday collections Sexton McMullen went to the
board of St. Paul's for permission "to sell $60.00 of Silver
Church Funds, at 3 per cent discount to enable him to
deposit the same in the Bank." The permission was granted.
To a generation familiar with war and wartime restrictions, it
should be hardly necessary to add that Mr. McMullen's transaction was effected on what we would call a black market.
The American war finally dragged to its two heart-breaking
climaxes—the surrender of General Robert E. Lee and the
assassination of President Abraham Lincoln. London in common with most Canadian cities and towns held a special
memorial service for the martyred president. It was an inter-
denominational service and was held not in the cathedral but
in the larger North Street Methodist Church one block east
on North Street (now Queens Avenue). Representatives of
all faiths took part in the service in the huge church (it
burned down in 1905), to the building of which St. Paul's
own millionaire, George Jervis Goodhue, had contributed
handsomely.

Legend has it that Goodhue's gift to the Methodists was
made for a political consideration, at a time when he needed
their support in his bid for an appointment to the Executive
Council of the Province of Canada (roughly comparable to
our present Senate). Whatever the truth of the story, shortly
after he made the gift he received the appointment and with
it the right to the prefix "Honourable." His allegiance to the
Church of England however never wavered and it was in
St. Paul's Cathedral that his daughter Maria Eliza was married in the hectic days of the American Civil War to Lieuten-
ant Hamilton Tovey of the Royal Engineers, one of the
well-placed young British officers who guarded Canada from
American democracy. As was mentioned earlier a son of this

The Very Reverend
George Mignon Innes

The Reverend Canon
Alfred George Dann

The Very Reverend
Louis Norman Tucker

The Very Reverend
Charles Edward Jeakins

The Very Reverend
Percival Nathaniel Harding

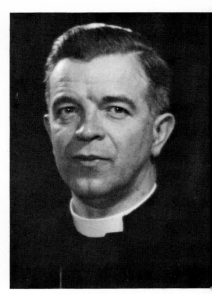

The Right Reverend
George Nasmith Luxton

The Very Reverend
Richard Charles Brown

The Very Reverend
Kenneth Bernard Keefe

marriage became commander of Britain's Home Fleet during World War Two.

It might have been thought that, with the war concluded and the reign of Mayor Cornish terminated, London would have been allowed to slip into the much-touted peace of the mid-period of Victoria's long sovereignty. Far from it. Other acts, other actors were waiting in the wings to make their contributions to the fevered drama of the 1860's.

One of the most vigorous actors was Archdeacon Isaac Hellmuth. Not content with carrying out, in an astonishingly short time, his bishop's wish for a theological college, he now turned to educational plans of his own devising. On October 17, 1864, the cornerstone was laid of a huge, 70-room boys' residential school called The London Collegiate Institute by the archdeacon, but known more familiarly and later, officially, as the Hellmuth Boys' School. The official opening took place on September 1, 1865. Although the school had a useful career of only twelve years, its influence on secondary school education in the province was far-reaching. The "collegiate institute" concept, with its emphasis on the classics, which Hellmuth had derived from German models, was copied by the Ontario Department of Education—without credit being given to Hellmuth.

The reluctance of Dr. Egerton Ryerson, director of the Ontario school system, to acknowledge his debt to the archdeacon is unfortunately typical of his contemporaries' reactions to Hellmuth and Hellmuth's ideas. It is true that Isaac Hellmuth drove others as he drove himself; it is true that in the pursuit of his own ideas he could be stubborn to the point of intransigeance; it is true that he often rode roughshod over the feelings of others and could not bring himself, even in Christian charity, to suffer fools gladly, but the great tragedy of this brilliant man's life lies in something much more basic and intellectually shocking than these human faults of character.

Isaac Hellmuth was a "converso," to use the Spanish term —a converted Jew. Furthermore he had that intellectual arrogance that so often characterizes the scholar of the Diaspora.

It is barely possible that his provincial Canadian contemporaries could have accepted a properly humble converso, but never one of such obvious intellectual attainments.

The very silence of his contemporaries and his later biographers in respect of these facts is in itself eloquent evidence of the ambivalent character of the community's reaction to the son of a Warsaw rabbi. Today, fifty years after his death, there is still a tendency among Londoners in speaking of Hellmuth to emphasize rather the fact that he was a former Jew than that he was the founder of the University of Western Ontario.

In fact he was, and still is, regarded as something of a freak —a sport, a graftling on the family tree of the Church of England in Canada. It is to this fact, disturbing as it may be to the good consciences of the descendants of the Anglo-Saxon founders of London, that the failure of Hellmuth's Canadian career must be attributed. His lonely and unequal battle ended, as it had to, in his defeat. The man who had a foot in each of two camps had a home in neither. Of him it could be said as of the Master he followed so faithfully: "Foxes have holes, and birds of the air have nests; but the Son of man hath not where to lay his head."

Defeat was still seventeen years distant in the spring of 1866 when the aging Bishop of Huron finally vacated the rectorship of St. Paul's which he had held for thirty-four years and appointed as rector and first Dean of Huron, the Venerable Archdeacon Isaac Hellmuth, principal of Huron College.

A new home having been found for the bishop in the South London suburbs, the big rectory on North Street was made ready for the new rector and his lady, a daughter of General Thomas Evans, C.B., of Three Rivers, Quebec, or Canada East, as it was then called. The churchwardens spent nearly $1,000 in making alterations and improvements to the rectory, but they must have been happy enough to do so, since the new rector declined any salary, preferring to give his services free.

As Hellmuth's assistant at the cathedral Bishop Cronyn named the Reverend G. M. Innes, the veteran of the stump episode and first rector of Christ Church. A cathedral chapter was named consisting of six canons—Innes himself, William

Bettridge, of Woodstock; E. L. Ellwood, of Goderich; Abraham Nelles, missionary to the Mohawks; J. C. Usher, of Brantford; and St. George Caulfield, of St. Thomas.

All these important changes must have seemed to the congregation of St. Paul's heralds of a new and infinitely more exciting era for the cathedral church of the diocese. Had they known what extravagant new ideas were about to blossom in the fertile mind of Isaac Hellmuth they might have been much less complacent about the bill for alterations to the rectory.

CHAPTER TEN

DEAN HELLMUTH

Then Isaac sowed in that land, and received in the same year an hundredfold: and the Lord blessed him.

Genesis 26: 12

Bishop Cronyn's action in appointing Archdeacon Hellmuth rector of the cathedral was not entirely his own idea, judging from a motion passed by a vestry meeting of April 2, 1866, over which the Reverend John McLean presided:

Moved by Mr. B. Shaw and sec'd by Mr. Wilson Mills: That in the opinion of the Vestry the spiritual & pecuniary interests of the Congregation of St. Paul's would be benefitted by the separation of the duties of Rector from those of the Bishop of the Diocese.

The feeling here expressed is understandable. The growing responsibilities of the episcopacy must have left the aging bishop, in spite of his seemingly boundless vigour, little time for the proper administration of his cathedral church. He was not slow in taking the hint; the new appointment came two months later.

Ordinarily the appointment of a new rector would have provided a pleasant ripple of excitement in the normally placid life of the cathedral. Coupled as it was with the departure of the popular young Mr. McLean to his new post as rector of St. John's Cathedral, Winnipeg, it could have been counted on to provide a topic of conversation for weeks. In the event however, both pieces of news were crowded out of the congregation's minds altogether by the extraordinary happenings of the first weeks of June.

Following the close of the American Civil War thousands of Irish veterans of both the Union and Confederate armies buried their differences in a mutually-acceptable antipathy to Great Britain which found its outlet in the maddest plan ever to be devised by the notably outlandish Irish mind.

Stated in the baldest terms, the Fenian Brotherhood plotted a mass assault on Canada, to liberate it "from the bondage of British oppression" and then use it either as a springboard for the invasion and liberation of Ireland from the B. of B.O. or as a hostage for the return of Ireland to the Irish.

The astonishing thing about the plot is that more than ten thousand Irishmen were silly enough to believe that it had a chance of succeeding. The Canadian government at first viewed the matter as a joke in somewhat bad taste but when the Irish began concentrating in thousands along the Niagara frontier as well as the St. Lawrence River and the border of New Brunswick in the first months of 1866, it was obvious the thing had to be taken seriously. The American government, from whose surplus war stores the Fenians had purchased tons of arms and ammunitions, was coldly unconcerned at the discomfiture of the British colonies.

By March the people of Canada West had stopped making jokes about the "Finnigans" and were in a state approaching panic. The government called up ten thousand militiamen and set them to drilling, often with ludicrously inadequate equipment. Merchants, businessmen and newspaper proprietors were seriously inconvenienced by the absence from their wonted places of clerks, runners and compositors of military age.

Nowhere in the province was the population more alarmed at the prospect of invasion than in London where for four years the people had lived in almost daily expectation of conquest by the victorious armies of the American Union. Nevertheless as the slow weeks dragged by without a sign of the threatened Fenian incursion, the jokes reappeared and fear was followed by irritation at the inconvenience caused by the government's apparently unnecessary action.

Belatedly, the United States government went through the motions of condemning the Fenian activity and *The London Free Press* expressed the hope that "we have nothing now to fear from these gasconading warriors." That was on May

30th. Two days later word arrived in London that the Fenian hordes in Buffalo, perhaps forced to the decision by the threat of the American government to intervene, were about to invade Canada. But the boy had cried "Wolf!" too often. Josiah Blackburn, editor and proprietor of *The Free Press,* as well as a valued member of the vestry of St. Paul's, expressed only intense irritation in his comment on the report:

Thieves and rogues all! We hope that this last sensation may die out without the country being put to the cost and inconvenience of a call to the volunteers; the whole farce is irritating enough, especially as our gallant fellows cannot get at the enemy!

The morning issue of the paper had scarcely been distributed to the subscribers than it was overtaken by a handbill "extra" announcing that a large force of Fenian raiders had landed at Fort Erie, on the Niagara border. Two additional extras followed containing no more certain information than that the Fenians were in Canada in undisclosed numbers and that the Canadian militia were converging on the scene.

At 1:30 P.M. the city council held a special meeting to consider forming a Home Guard for the defence of the city. Mayor David Glass (Frank Cornish's old enemy) reported that the commandant of the British garrison had assured him that two thousand stand of arms could be made available for this purpose. It was agreed to send a telegram to Lord Monck, the Governor-General, asking his advice. Lord Monck replied promptly, assuring the council that the action was unnecessary and that the situation was under control. Accordingly the council decided to organize a Home Guard.

That was Friday, June 1st.

On Saturday a call went out to every militiaman "left in the city" to report at once to the militia barracks. Meanwhile the city's greybeards were organized into Home Guard companies with whatever equipment could be begged, borrowed or liberated. One alderman bought two pistols, one for each hip, thoughtfully charging the cost to the city council.

News from the front was virtually non-existent, although *The Free Press* had a correspondent, Malcolm Bremner, in the field. A report from Port Stanley brought spine-chilling news that a fleet of more than thirty schooners, believed to be carrying supplies for the Fenians, had been sighted on Lake Erie.

Sunday was a day of massive community jitters, climaxed by the most dramatic single event in the entire history of St. Paul's. The big church was packed for the eleven o'clock service—an automatic community response to danger in 1866 as it was to the so-called "Cuban crisis" in 1962. Many of the men in the congregation carried sidearms. William Hayman, late of Devonshire, England, was there along with the men of the 53rd Regiment of Foot, especially despatched to Canada and to London as a result of the Fenian threat. Mr. Hayman, who later settled in London and became a prominent contractor, left a graphic account of the atmosphere in the cathedral that Sunday and for several Sundays during the summer of 1866:

Many a Sunday I have gone to St. Paul's Church with my rifle on my shoulder and forty rounds of ball ammunition in my cartridge pouch, expecting to have to fight my way back from the church to the barracks.

The service was coming to a close—and we can be sure that the prayer for peace was said with special fervour that morning—when the city fire bell at Covent Garden Market two blocks away began clanging furiously. It was the prearranged invasion signal.

Before the galvanized congregation could rise to their feet the doors of the narthex burst open and a uniformed bugler, followed by two drummers appeared and marched down the aisle blowing and banging away at the call to arms.

The speed with which the church was emptied would have done credit to a grade-school fire drill. Utter pandemonium reigned outside as each uninformed parishioner asked his equally uninformed neighbour what it was all about and relayed the resulting misinformation to the latest arrival.

It appeared that some unimpeachable source had reported that the Fenians had crossed the St. Clair River, seized Sarnia and were marching on London. One rumour had them only ten miles away. All the reports were false but the citizenry had no way of knowing, for news of the actual events on the Niagara frontier was totally lacking, whether through military censorship or just plain bad communications, it is impossible now to say.

All that summer Sunday afternoon haggard Londoners walked the downtown streets, haunting the offices of the three daily newspapers—*The Free Press, The Advertiser* and *The Prototype*—for a scrap of genuine information. The news finally arrived at 4 P.M. Since it was a Sunday, no extras were printed but all three newspapers placed bulletins in front of their buildings. There had been a sharp skirmish between the Fenians and the militia, with casualties on both sides. The Fenians were in full retreat across the border.

Only later was the full story of the Fenian fiasco revealed. The Irish leader had neglected to provide himself with adequate maps of the area, became lost, engaged the militia almost accidentally and after a tragi-comic battle in which seven Canadians and six Fenians were killed, retreated precipitately across the Niagara River with his entire invasion force.

That was the high-water mark of the Fenian "invasion." There were other, smaller raids at various points along the borders of British North America over a period of several months, but the security of the provinces was at no time seriously threatened.

The raids however achieved what the purely theoretical danger of American conquest had been unable to accomplish. The reluctant politicians of Canada East, Canada West, Nova Scotia and New Brunswick speedily decided on the advantages of the union proposal they had been debating for more than three years. The British North America Act was hustled through the British House of Commons, approved by the Lords and endorsed by the Queen. In July, 1867, the Dominion of Canada came into being.

There is no direct reference to this special day in the records of St. Paul's Cathedral. A. G. Smyth, clerk of the vestry of St. Paul's was perhaps a little self-conscious as he wrote the unfamiliar, "London, *Ontario,*" at the head of the next set of minutes. The board met the day after the holiday but their minutes are all business. The churchwardens issued a cheque for $85.84 to cover the payment of seven accounts including that of Mr. Oldburn, bellows blower, who received

$10 for pumping air into the organ for three months of
Sundays.

There were also two applications received—from Mrs.
Henderson and Mr. Shaw—for "General Burrows' pew
vacated by him" but the churchwardens were informed that
the Dean "had bespoken it previously for Major Simpson,
commanding the Battery." The American Civil War and the
Fenian raids were over and Canada a new nation, but London's civilians still had to take second place to the British
Army. It was another two years before the London garrison
was closed and the troops returned to England.

Meanwhile Dean Hellmuth was vigorously engaged in
effecting changes. In spite of the continued efforts of the congregation, the debt on the church had grown rather than
diminished, to a record total of $14,801 in April, 1866.
Nevertheless the church continually had to expand its facilities to meet the needs of a growing community. The old
schoolhouse, once used for refugee Negroes and latterly as a
Sunday School and meeting hall, had become totally inadequate. At the same time the Diocese of Huron was without
offices and had been operating out of the cathedral rectory.
And so, in 1866, the first steps were taken jointly by the
cathedral and the diocese to erect a new brick building on
the northwest corner of the cathedral property to provide
offices for the Church Society and school rooms for St. Paul's
Sunday School "and other church purposes." The building
was completed in 1868 and named in honour of the bishop,
Cronyn Hall. Its successor building carries the same name.
The old schoolhouse was sold for $100 and moved to Central
Avenue, where it was converted to a residence. The site on
which it had stood was sold a few years later to the federal
government.

The churchwardens soon discovered that their new rector
was a man of action and singleness of purpose, quite capable
of carrying out a plan on his own and only later informing
them of what he had done. This was the case with the small
mortuary chapel and caretaker's house which he caused to be
built in 1867 in St. Paul's Cemetery. The vestry was informed after the event and agreed to repay the dean out of

cemetery funds. When the cemetery was closed, ten years later, the chapel was moved to a site on Dundas Street, between Egerton and Eva streets, where it housed the first congregation of St. Matthew's Church.

The cemetery had by now become a favourite place of resort for the people of London, on week days as well as on Sundays. With its pleasant walks, flower beds and well-placed trees, it served the purpose of a community park, as yet lacking in the city. The Victorians, not suffering from their descendants' grossly-exaggerated cult of the dead, found nothing morbid in the living taking their pleasures amid the graves of their ancestors.

Indeed the cemetery became so popular with all classes and types, including inevitably a few town rowdies, that the vestry was obliged to establish a set of rules governing the public's use of the cemetery. Some of the prohibitions are very revealing:

No. 1. The gates will be closed at sunset each day.

No. 2. No admission on Sundays or holidays except by ticket. Tickets to be furnished on application to the Church-wardens at their discretion. One ticket will admit the holder and friends.

No. 3. No vehicle to be driven faster than a walk.

No. 4. Vehicles accompanying funerals (except such as contain chief mourners) to be fastened outside to posts provided for this purpose.

No. 5. No persons carrying refreshments to be admitted within the grounds.

No. 6. Picking of flowers is strictly prohibited.

No. 7. No smoking is permitted and no dogs are allowed within the grounds.

No. 8. No children admitted unless accompanied by Parents or other suitable Persons.

No. 9. Any person disturbing the quiet and good order of the place will be compelled instantly to leave the grounds.

No. 10. The Superintendent and those acting under him are required to carry all regulations into effect.

Here, alas, we can see Victorian conformity beginning to establish its stranglehold over the free and easy ways of the one-time frontier city. Not that London's nonconformists had passed away—far from it—but their numbers had shrunk; they were no longer the majority.

One group of arch-nonconformists provided the city's biggest sensation of 1867—bigger by far than the tame fireworks of the first Dominion Day and only slightly less exciting than the Fenian raids.

They were called the Hellfriar Club, in imitation of a more famous group of English fun-raisers. The club's membership included a number of bored young London intellectuals and a few British Army officers of the same age and general attainments. They relieved their boredom by writing, printing and distributing secretly throughout the city, broadsheets satirizing the actions of their elders. The militia companies hastily organized at the time of the *Trent* incident for instance, were mercilessly lampooned in a Hellfriar effort called "The Magenta Rangers" and another vicious little effort poked well-earned fun at the Home Guard of 1866. "But," one of them said many years later, "the people who got it worst were the mushroom aristocracy. They could hardly sleep at night for fear next morning they would be posted all over the city." (In passing it must be pointed out in all justice that the scions of one London generation of mushroom aristocracy have always been the bitterest opponents of the following generation's nouveaux riche.)

It was at some time following the Fenian scare that two members of the Hellfriar Club, over a convivial glass, made a fantastic wager. It was not the amount of the wager that was fantastic, but the subject of the bet. One of the participants was to enter a given number of London homes, by night, in the course of a year and successfully elude capture by the police. Since "break and enter" was not entirely an unknown offence even in the 1860's it was agreed that each entry was to be made in some idiosyncratic manner so as to identify it as the work of the participant in the wager.

And so it was that the year 1867 was marked by the weirdest series of house-breakings in the city's history. Early in the game the city's press applied the name "Slippery Jack" to the unknown marauder and Londoners followed his career with bated breaths. "Slippery Jack" stole nothing; his sole object was entering homes by night and making it obvious that he alone was the author of the deed.

"Slippery Jack" was reduced to many expedients to ensure the knowledge of his identity. He discovered that Londoners, in spite of their professed fear of his depredations, were exceedingly sound sleepers. Sometimes he would awaken the head of the house by shaking him or shouting in his ear. At other times he would pile the furniture in the middle of a room or turn it all upside down. Or, if there were comely young ladies in the house he would tickle their bare feet until they woke up.

The wager was won in spite of the frenzied efforts of the police force and a young army of citizen volunteers. "Slippery Jack" then announced, via the columns of the city's newspapers, that he was prepared to meet any legitimate bill for damages against him. He took the precaution of pointing out that he had a list of the homes he had entered and knew approximately what material damage he had caused.

Then, having collected his hard-won wager, he took his accustomed place the following Sunday in the pews reserved for army officers at St. Paul's Cathedral. Shortly after he returned to England with his regiment, later to assume his father's estates and his father's peerage.

After "Slippery Jack" and the demise of the Hellfriar Club life in London became relatively tame. Not that there was a scarcity of incident, for there was not; but the sting and the drama of the formative years was gone forever.

In 1869 St. Paul's vestry decided on a step that had been in contemplation for some time. The necessary motion was passed at a special meeting on May 5:

That an assessment of 50% the payment of which to extend over two years be made upon the Pews to enable the Churchwardens to enlarge the Chancel, to paint the Pews & clean & colour the walls . . . The cost of the above Improvements not to exceed $3,500.00.

Considering the small amount paid out, the alterations were quite extensive. The tiny "half-octagonal" chancel that projected at the rear of the original church like a woman's bustle was removed and a new, square chancel was built, some thirty-eight feet in depth. A vestry was added to the north of the chancel and an organ gallery to the south.

During the few months that the repairs took, the congregation worshipped on Sundays in the auditorium of the city hall on Richmond Street. For this kindness the city council received a nicely-worded vote of thanks and a cheque for $37.95 to cover janitorial service and the cost of gas lighting.

By herculean efforts the cathedral's debt had been reduced by some $3,000 in spite of these additional costs, but it was still a long way from being liquidated. Until it was, the principal church in the diocese could not be consecrated. A select committee of vestry was appointed in April, 1871, to establish a fund to retire the debt from among the members of the congregation.

Meanwhile the life of the doughty founder of the Diocese of Huron was ebbing. In September, 1869, Bishop Cronyn was well enough to welcome Prince Arthur of Connaught (later H.R.H. the Duke of Connaught, one of Canada's best-liked governors-general) when the Prince came to London to open Hellmuth Ladies' College, the third of the indefatigable dean's adventures in higher education. The following year was not a good one for him however, and at the synod of June, 1871, he asked for assistance in carrying out the heavy duties of the episcopacy.

The bishop's request came as a great shock to many old friends who having seen him carry on a vigorous priesthood in his adopted home for nearly forty years could well be excused for considering Benjamin Cronyn not only tireless, but timeless as well.

A special synod was convened on July 19, 1871. The names of five candidates for the office of coadjutor Bishop of Huron were advanced, but only one ballot was necessary. Dean Hellmuth received fifty-three votes from the clergy and seventy-eight from the laity. On St. Bartholomew's Day, August 24, he was consecrated at St. Paul's Cathedral as Bishop of Norfolk with the right of succession.

He bore the title for a few weeks only. Bishop Cronyn died at the See House in South London on September 22, in his seventieth year. His funeral took place three days later. The late Dr. Crowfoot's account of the obsequies can hardly be improved upon:

> His funeral . . . was long remembered as one of the most impressive ever seen in London. The clergy of the diocese, with the Bishop of Norfolk at their head, assembled at the See House and headed the procession to the cathedral. The mayor and aldermen followed as a tribute of respect . . . The staff and students of Huron College were there to do honour to their founder. The members of the school board and the teachers from the public schools were present to pay tribute to one who had been a member of the school board since its inception, and had consistently refused to accept any remuneration for his services, preferring that any money he might be entitled to receive should be spent in prizes for the encouragement of learning. It is impossible to enumerate others who were present. It is enough to say that the whole city was there.

Isaac Hellmuth returned from the funeral to his new home, Norwood House adjacent to Hellmuth Ladies' College, as the second Bishop of Huron. His boundless energy now hit its full stride. One of his first actions was to merge the old Church Society and the Synod of Huron into a single body—the Incorporated Synod of the Diocese of Huron. A second step was to name the Reverend Canon G. M. Innes rector of St. Paul's Cathedral. The office of Dean of Huron he reserved for Dr. Michael Boomer, his successor as principal of Huron College. On Dr. Boomer's death in 1888, Canon Innes was appointed third Dean of Huron.

The new bishop then turned to the consideration of his cathedral church—with startling results. At a special meeting of St. Paul's vestry held exactly one month after Bishop Cronyn's death, Bishop Hellmuth introduced Canon Innes as the new rector and then dropped his bombshell. It was his wish, he said:

> that a memorial should be erected to the memory of our late reverend Diocesan, Bishop Cronyn, in the form of a Cathedral Church for this Diocese to be built in London and of his great desire that the congregation of St. Paul's through their Vestry should assist him by heading the list with a subscription of $2,000.00 payable in three or four years as the Vestry should see fit.

It has been said by those who knew him that Bishop Hellmuth was a most eloquent and persuasive person. The records of St. Paul's certainly bear this out. At a special meeting of the vestry held on November 6 the following motion was put and carried unanimously:

Moved by Mr. J. B. Strathy
Sec'd by Mr. Hamilton

Resolved, that whereas his Lordship the Bishop of Huron has intimated his intention to erect within this City a Cathedral Church in memory of our revered and lamented Bishop, the late Benjamin Cronyn, D.D., and whereas the Bishop of Huron whilst Rector of St. Paul's declined to receive any stipend whatever or assistance towards supplying the necessary clerical ministrations of the Church out of its funds in order that the debt thereon might be liquidated as speedily as possible and there being a probability that the debt of the church will be shortly paid: It is desirable as a mark of respect to the late Bishop as well as to our late Rector and also to exhibit our regard for the interest of the Church in this Diocese that this Vestry appropriate out of the Pew Rents Four Thousand Dollars towards the erection of the proposed Cathedral, the same to be payable Five Hundred Dollars at the time of Breaking Ground and Five Hundred Dollars in each succeeding year.

When the vestry next met, at Easter, 1872, the veteran clerk, A. G. Smyth, who for thirteen years had "meticulously dated his minutes" at "St. Paul's Cathedral" headed them instead "St. Paul's *Church*".

CHAPTER ELEVEN

DEBT

There was a certain creditor which had two debtors: the one owed five hundred pence, and the other fifty. And when they had nothing to pay, he frankly forgave them both.

Luke 7: 41-42

It was predictable that Bishop Hellmuth's proposal to build a new cathedral would meet with opposition from the congregation of St. Paul's, and the storm was not long in breaking. Compounding the situation was the bishop's reference to the new cathedral as a "memorial" to the life of Bishop Cronyn. Unfortunately for Hellmuth the late bishop's family had decided shortly after his death to build a new church some blocks east of St. Paul's as a permanent memorial to Dr. Cronyn. This church, at the corner of Queens Avenue and William Street was turned over to its congregation on December 13, 1873, free and clear of all debt, by the surviving members of the family. It has ever since been called the Bishop Cronyn Memorial Church.

As soon as the intentions of the Cronyns were made known to him, Bishop Hellmuth dropped the "memorial" aspect of his proposed cathedral, but the fat was already in the fire. At the Easter vestry meeting of 1872 Charles Hutchinson, Middlesex county crown attorney, and B. Shaw authored a resolution which illustrated the growing resentment of a section at least of the congregation:

That inasmuch as the vote of the last Vestry of $4,000 to the Cathedral Building Fund was granted on the understanding that the said Cathedral was intended as a Memorial to the late Bishop and partly as a recognition of the late Rector's services and whereas it is alleged that the said Cathedral will not be such Memorial Church and this Vestry desire notwithstanding to carry out the intentions of the last Vestry in recognizing the said services of our late Rector, be it resolved that this Vestry vote the sum of $2,000 to the Cathedral fund in yearly payments of $500 each.

A justifiable amendment to the motion suggesting that the Bishop himself should be present if any change in the original resolution were to be contemplated carried, and the motion was lost.

There was a much larger attendance than usual at the adjourned vestry meeting two weeks later and everyone came loaded for bear. There was a perfunctory passage of accounts, the lord bishop was formally invited to attend the business of the meeting and then Mr. Hutchinson rose to present an expanded resolution. He had a different seconder this time— G. F. Jewell. The resolution simply called for the rescinding, in toto, of the $4,000 vote "for the following principal reasons":

1. That the Vestry ought not to have authorized any charge upon the pew rents for a purpose not connected with the interests of St. Paul's Church.

2. That the grant in question is for a purpose not connected with and adverse to the interests of St. Paul's Church.

3. That the Vestry by such resolution undertook to impose a charge upon the future income of the Church over which it had no right of control.

An amendment was promptly moved by James Hamilton and Lieut. Col. John Walker, repeating the terms of the original vestry grant but "omitting all words having a memorial reference." After what the minutes refer to as "considerable discussion" the vote on the amendment was taken. It carried, by a vote of twenty-six to fourteen.

Bishop Hellmuth then thanked the vestry for the grant but declined to receive it under the circumstances. His calling, he said, "was that of a Peace Maker" and he did not wish to see "any feeling of discord amongst any congregation in the Diocese over which he presided." He then pronounced his blessing impartially on both groups of belligerents and the meeting adjourned.

If the Crown Attorney and the thirteen others who voted with him thought that by their opposition they could scotch the cathedral plans of their bishop, they only proved that they did not know Isaac Hellmuth. The cornerstone of Holy Trinity Cathedral was laid a few weeks later, on June 6, 1872, as the highlight of the new bishop's first synod.

The massive stone building which was officially opened on November 2, 1873, at a cost of $27,000 was not the cathedral proper, but merely the Chapter House which was later to be joined to the cathedral by a cloister. The architect's plans showed a huge, cruciform Gothic church flanked by a spire. As has rightly been said, one has only to look at the great stone mass of the Chapter House which still stands on Piccadilly Street near Richmond Street, to realize how much the cathedral complex would have cost. Like so many of Isaac Hellmuth's dreams, neither the times nor the place were right for it.

Meanwhile in the same week that the cornerstone of the new cathedral was laid, the bishop's chief opponent among the congregation of St. Paul's was having problems of his own.

On June 4, 1872, two men forcibly abducted James Simpson near Hellmuth's Boys' School, forced him into a cab and drove off to the Grand Trunk Railway station.

Within a few days it became known that the kidnapped man was actually Dr. James Rufus Bratton, of Yorkville, South Carolina, wanted by the United States government for Ku Klux Klan activities, including the murder of a Negro, and that his kidnappers were an agent of the United States Secret Service and Charles Hutchinson's deputy, Isaac Bell Cornwall. The agent had successfully transported Bratton across the international border at Windsor, representing him as a dangerous lunatic under restraint.

The resulting international uproar spreading out from its focal point in London, Ontario, to the embassies of London, Ottawa and Washington, brought Great Britain and the United States closer to the brink of war than at any time since the close of the War of 1812-1814. Fortunately the crisis was not prolonged. The United States government backed down from an initially hard-headed stand and returned Dr. Bratton to London on July 17, in time for him to appear as a witness at the trial of Isaac Bell Cornwall.

Cornwall was given three years in penitentiary and Dr. Bratton set up practice in London under his proper name. And, after all the excitement was over, Crown Attorney Hutchinson transferred his allegiance from St. Paul's Church to the new church of St. James (Westminster) which had been begun as a mission in the Askin street school by Mrs. Benjamin Cronyn, the late bishop's second wife, shortly before his death. Services had been conducted there by Canon G. M. Innes, rector of the cathedral.

St. James' was one of four daughters of St. Paul's born in the decade of the 1870's. The congregation of St. John the Evangelist was organized in this period, meeting in Huron College chapel and the Chapter House until their church in North London was built, in 1887/88. St. George's Church, in London West, began as a mission in 1874. St. Luke's on the Hamilton road, not to be confused with the present church of the same name in London North, later became All Saints' Church. All four churches received financial and other assistance in their formative years from the mother church.

The mother church herself was having continuing grave financial difficulties. Nothing the congregation could do seemed to have the slightest effect in reducing the debt which hovered consistently between $10,000 and $15,000. On one occasion it was discovered that the churchwardens had been called on personally to assume some $5,000 of the church's "floating indebtedness."

Costs, quite naturally, kept rising in spite of the prolonged financial depression which gripped the entire country following the repeal by the Americans of the Reciprocity Treaty in 1866. In 1873 St. Paul's old organ was sold for $1,000, but it cost $5,000 to replace it. Salaries kept rising. When Mrs. Raymond resigned her post as organist in 1877, her yearly salary had risen to $300 from the original $100 and the new organist, George B. Sippi, started at $500.

The salaries paid to the various assistants to the rector kept rising too, nor were these men always easy to obtain and to keep, judging from the procession of names passing through the records. From 1866 to 1891, eleven clergymen served St. Paul's for varying periods: the Reverend S. B. Kellogg, 1866; the Reverend G. L. Low, 1867; the Reverend G. M. Innes, 1868; the Reverend Reginald Heber Starr, 1868; the Reverend A. C. Hill (later rector of St. Thomas and Archdeacon of Elgin), 1869-1871; the Reverend W. H. Tilley (later first rector of Bishop Cronyn Memorial Church, who died in 1878), 1871-1873; the Reverend J. G. Baylis (later a canon in the Diocese of Montreal), 1873; the Reverend H. F. Darnell, 1874; the Reverend J. Gemley, 1874-1878; the Reverend Alfred Brown, 1878-1884 and the Reverend R. Hicks, 1885-1891.

By the time Mr. Gemley arrived the salary of the assistant had risen to $1,250 and by the time the popular Mr. Brown left the finances of the church were in such a parlous state that Canon Innes decided to carry on for a year by himself, in order to save money. One year was enough for the canon. At the end of that time he reported to the vestry that he had paid 1,071 visits, officiated at 43 funerals, preached 147 sermons and held 67 week-day services. In addition he had provided a chaplaincy service for the City Hospital, the Middlesex County Gaol and the Asylum for the Insane.

The veteran sexton, Thomas McMullen, resigned in 1873 and was succeeded by John Ferns who served the church until 1881 when the vestry appointed Laurence Pinnell who was to surpass McMullen's twenty-one years of service.

The humdrum 1870's ended with some mild excitement for the Anglicans of London. In 1878 Bishop Hellmuth capped his career by spearheading the founding of the University of Western Ontario, his last and greatest accomplishment in the field of higher education. Here again the brilliant educationist was ahead of his times and it was not until the good bishop lay on his deathbed nearly a quarter of a century later that the floundering little institution in London, Ontario, began gathering its strength for the tremendous future that lay ahead of it.

The last big event of the decade looked at first like a major calamity for the congregation of St. Paul's. In June, 1879, the corporation of the village of London East informed the rector and wardens that a bye-law was about to be passed prohibiting interments within the municipality and that in consequence "St. Paul's Cemetery will be closed forthwith."

The site that in 1849 had seemed safely outside the city limits had been swallowed up by the expanding city and its industrial suburb of London East. By 1879 the cemetery was hemmed in by residences and tall factory chimneys. The move would have had to be made in time; the action of the municipality merely gave it a deadline.

A special committee of vestry was set up and proceeded immediately to the search for a new site. By the middle of August they were able to report success. A most felicitous location on the banks of the Thames River two or three miles west of the city had been secured at a price just under $10,000. It consisted of fifty-six acres—subsequently expanded to seventy-eight acres. Part of the property, previously owned by William Blinn, had been known as "Woodland Park" and so the name "Woodland" was applied to the cemetery.

The removal of the bodies from the old cemetery was a gigantic undertaking that occupied several weeks. Some of the uneasy corpses were enduring their second removal, having previously been taken from the old churchyard to the Dundas Street site. Most of the removals were effected by wagon but at one stage owing to a scarcity of such vehicles a fleet of local hansom cabs was pressed into service. The resulting uproar by the cab-using public occupied the "Letters to the Editor" columns of the local newspapers for weeks.

Many of the bodies—paupers and victims of the savage epidemics of the 1840's and 1850's—lay in unmarked graves and were left behind inadvertently, as always happens in such cases. For years afterwards human bones turned up whenever a foundation was dug in the old cemetery grounds.

The sale of the former property eventually tipped the scales in the efforts of the congregation of St. Paul's to liquidate the church's debt but since many of the sales were made on a time-payment basis it was a few years before the effects were truly noted.

The new cemetery was opened and in use in time to receive fifty-one bodies, victims of the most tragic disaster in London's history. On May 24, 1881, the river steamer *Victoria* overturned on the Thames River west of London opposite Woodland Cemetery spilling its load of more than six hundred holiday-makers into the water. The total number of victims was never ascertained accurately but estimates ranged as high as two hundred and fifteen. Funeral processions to the five London cemeteries followed one another in a seemingly endless stream for a week.

There is probably not one of the older London churches without at least one memorial to a victim of the *Victoria* disaster. There are two memorials in St. Paul's Cathedral, one to a victim, one to a survivor. The alms bason in the sanctuary carries an inscription which reads:

A thank-offering to Almighty God by Marion Grace Barker, saved from the wreck of the steamer *Victoria*, 24th May, 1881.

A memorial window on the north side of the nave commemorates John Walsingham Cooke Meredith who, at seventy-two, was the most elderly victim of the tragedy. The father of a brilliant family one of whom became a chief justice, he was one of the two most illustrious victims of the disaster, the other being William McBride, sixty-four, a former mayor of the city.

The decade which for London had begun luridly with the savage murder of five members of the family of James Donnelly in Biddulph Township, sixteen miles north of the city and continued with the needless horror of the *Victoria*, was not yet finished ravishing the city with tragedy. On July 11, 1883, after a series of torrential rainstorms, a flash flood on the north branch of the Thames River roared across the suburb of London West in the middle of the night smashing homes and businesses and causing thirteen deaths. The loss of life might have been greater had it not been for the warning given by a reporter for *The London Advertiser* who made a detour to check the height of the river on his way back to the office from a disastrous fire which had destroyed a large oil refinery in London East.

In the midst of these catastrophes the resignation from his office of the second Bishop of Huron seemed almost an anticlimax. In the summer of 1883 Bishop Hellmuth gave up his one-man struggle to remake his adopted city educationally, culturally and ecclesiastically and vacated his see. The choice of the special synod called to elect his successor was the Very Reverend Maurice Scollard Baldwin, Dean of Montreal.

For four more years the Chapter House continued to be the cathedral—or more technically, pro-cathedral—of the diocese. The final quietus to Bishop Hellmuth's plans for Holy Trinity was administered when the Canadian Pacific Railway right of way was driven through London immediately to the south of the Chapter House.

The building of the CPR began in 1885, the year of the outbreak of the Riel Rebellion. London's own 7th Fusiliers Regiment—whose tattered battle standard now hangs in St. Paul's Cathedral—travelled to the Northwest via the new railway. There was some initial difficulty in rounding up the regiment for the journey. The call up was given by a bugler bouncing franctically over the rutted streets of London on a penny-farthing bicycle in the early morning hours of April 1, 1885. Many of the regiment's personnel, hearing the wild tooting, remembered the date and mildly cursing the April-Fool joker, rolled over and went back to sleep.

They got going eventually and arrived at the scene of the fighting to discover it was all over. After a few weeks on the prairies they turned and came back again without ever having fired a shot in anger. The city council gave them a great reception.

The CPR line to London was officially opened in June, 1887. On the 8th of that month a special meeting of the vestry of St. Paul's Church was convened to consider the contents of a letter received by Canon Innes from Verschoyle

Cronyn, son of the former bishop, chancellor of the diocese since 1859 and president of London's recently-organized horse-drawn street railway system. The letter read:

I am requested by His Lordship the Bishop of Huron to say that he desires to establish his Chair in St. Paul's Church if this meets your wishes and those of your Vestry. On receiving an affirmative reply, I shall be prepared to submit conditions for such an arrangement.

After ten years as a parish church, St. Paul's was about to become once more the cathedral church of the Diocese of Huron.

CHAPTER TWELVE

DEDICATION

By virtue of the sacred office committed to us in the Church, I do declare to be consecrated and set apart from all profane and common uses this House of God under the Name and Title of the Church of St. Paul; in the Name of the Father, and of the Son, and of the Holy Ghost. Amen.

The Prayer of Consecration

The financial problems under which the congregation of St. Paul's had laboured for so many years were finally solved in 1884 largely through the sale of lands belonging to the church. The long-delayed service of consecration was celebrated by Bishop Baldwin on November 12, 1884.

The dedication of the church after thirty-eight years in an economic wilderness acted on the congregation like a tonic. All departments of the church were revitalized. When consecration was followed by the removal of the bishop's chair to its former position in the old diocesan mother church, the congregation's energy knew no bounds. When a proposal was made for the building of a new vestry, thirteen persons subscribed a total of $515 on the spot. Before they had finished the project had grown into a massive face-lifting for the whole cathedral complex.

If the financial climate was good for the cathedral, it was not for the cathedral's community. The long economic depression which had begun in the early 1870's was only just reaching its peak. Poverty was the lot of an increasing number of townspeople, in the labouring classes particularly.

The congregation, which hitherto had tended to dissociate itself from the distress apparent all around it, contenting itself with an occasional special collection for the poor and a perfunctory pat on the back for the rector and his assistant for their work in this field, now got into the act itself. As is so often the case, the inspiration for the social welfare work

125

of the church came very largely from the women of the congregation.

In the fall of 1885 an organization meeting was held of the St. Paul's Church Workers' Association to plan "the work of the Church among the poor" for the winter. The parish was divided into sixteen districts and twenty-five women visitors appointed whose job was to "investigate the circumstances of those in need, and obtain for them the help required." Among the visitors may be found the names of many London families long connected with the cathedral and with the life of the community in general. One notes the names of Miss Westcott and Mrs. G. B. Harris, families whose connections with downtown Ridout Street lasted for more than a century; Mrs. Talbot Macbeth, Mrs. E. B. Reed, Mrs. W. J. Reid and Mrs. De la Hooke among many others.

The CWA worked strictly with the poor of its own church and operated four sub-committees:

The Dorcas and Relief Committee. This committee met every Thursday afternoon from two to four o'clock and was responsible for making clothing for the poor and distributing relief. Its first report, presented in April, 1886, gives an interesting view of the committee's method of operation:

When the winter set in and it became necessary to give relief in food and fuel to the needy members of the congregation, it was decided that the groceries should be purchased wholesale, and distributed to applicants upon signed orders from the visitors of the respective districts . . . The plan proved very satisfactory, and a large amount of relief has been given at comparatively small cost. Forty-seven orders have been filled by a supply of nourishing food. Fuel has been obtained when possible from the (municipal) Relief Inspector, and only in cases where it could not be thus obtained was it purchased on a recommendation from the district visitor.

Food supplies purchased by the committee consisted entirely of staples such as oatmeal, rice, tea, sugar and "biscuits." Fuel, materials for clothing and rent absorbed the greater part of the $257 spent in a six-month period. Of this, $116 was laid out in assisting poor persons to pay their rent, by monthly or weekly allowances. It was noted that Mrs. Lamb—"over ninety-four years of age"—received a half dollar a week for this purpose.

Mothers' Meetings and Provident Society. This group had apparently existed prior to the formation of the CWA. In the winter of 1885/86 a total of thirty-eight women were enabled "to obtain good clothing by their own needlework." In that period two hundred and sixty garments were made, the value of which to the members was "continually expressed by them in terms of sincerest gratitude to the lady managers." The "managers" were Mrs. E. W. Hyman and Mrs. W. J. Reid. "Profitable and instructive books" were read to the members at each weekly meeting, which always closed with religious exercises.

St. Paul's Branch of the Girls' Friendly Society. This group also had had a prior existence. Its work was with young women, particularly with newcomers to the community, its object being "to provide a home that can be resorted to by the members when out of employment, and thus avoid the temptations to which many are exposed." The Society did not have any notable success in the beginning; its membership rarely rose above ten.

St. Paul's Sewing Class. This group began its operations in February, 1885, the object being "to teach those children to sew whose mothers have not time to teach them at home." At first sight this does not seem an especially attractive proposition, but thirty-six youngsters were enrolled in the first year. It may be that the mothers who did not have time to teach their offspring to sew were in the market for a free baby-sitting service.

On paper, the work carried on by the St. Paul's Church Workers' Association and its four sub-committees strikes a surprisingly modern note and parallels to a remarkable degree the work of the Core Area Project launched by the congregation in 1963. (See Chapter Fifteen.) However, there is little real resemblance between the social work philosophies of the 1880's and the 1960's. The relationship of the "lady managers" to those being helped was strongly influenced by the mid-Victorian pattern of the parochial Lady Bountiful graciously distributing baskets of good things to the "deserving

poor." It was still to be many years before the modern principles of social rehabilitation would be established whereby
all distressed persons are helped to help themselves.

The work of the CWA continued for many years until the
development of government-sponsored relief agencies and
private charitable organizations rendered its functions, apparently, redundant. The rise in recent years of a new class of
"invisible poor" in the central parts of all Canadian cities has
again focussed the attention of downtown churches on the
mute problems waiting on their very doorsteps.

The explosion of congregational energy that found a flesh-
and-blood outlet in the work of the Church Workers' Association, expressed itself in monumental works of stone, brick
and steel as well. As a first, small step, the picket fence in
front of the cathedral which had become old and rotten, was
replaced by the present stone and iron fence in 1887. The
fence was brought at a bargain price of $250 from the Cana-
dian government. It had previously enclosed the grounds
occupied by the Customs House (now the headquarters
building of the Western Ontario Area, Canadian Army).

Five years later the cathedral congregation embarked on its
most ambitious building project since the completion of the
church in 1846. To give the church true "cathedral proportions" the chancel built by Bishop Hellmuth in 1869 was
razed, together with the easternmost bay of the 1846 building. On the ground thus cleared the present wide transepts
and spacious chancel and apse were built. The old side
galleries were removed and an elaborate system of roof beams
was devised so as to make all pillars unnecessary.

At the same time the brick building at the northwest corner
of the cathedral grounds which had served as church and
synod offices since 1868 was pulled down and a new Cronyn
Hall erected, extending northward from the new chancel. A
striking feature of the new building was a great hall seventy-
six feet long and thirty-eight feet wide with a huge stained-
glass window facing on Richmond Street. A tower built in
the same style as the cathedral tower and a four-arch cloister
connecting with the choir vestry completed the picture of the
cathedral complex as viewed from the front. The interior of

the building contained offices for the synod as well as the cathedral offices.

The total cost of the changes which totally altered the appearance of the church both inside and out was $60,000—four times the cost of the original church.

Bishop Baldwin, considered one of the most eloquent preachers of a period in the history of the Canadian church noted for its preaching, officiated at the re-opening of the cathedral on April 8, 1894. His text was from II Timothy 2: 19—"Nevertheless the foundations of God standeth sure."

A large brass tablet on the west wall of the cathedral in the narthex commemorates the justifiable pride of the congregation in its accomplishment.

Meanwhile the city's long Victorian summer was drawing to a close. In England the Widow of Windsor had celebrated the jubilee of her reign (1887) with pomp and circumstance outdoing the triumphs of the Caesars. In her most parochial dominion, Canada, the winds of change were fitfully and decorously stirring the skirts of destiny. With agonizing slowness the nation was beginning to shake the grip of the long depression. London was growing, slowly, partly by natural increase, partly by the annexation of its suburban areas. In 1885 the village of London East then as now the city's principal industrial area was annexed. Five years later the residential suburbs which together made up the section loosely described as London South were added to the city and in 1898 the village of London West or Petersville became a part of the city. These additions brought the population figure at the turn of the century to just under 40,000.

To this sprawling amalgamation of municipalities came progress, to be greeted with characteristic reluctance. The first commercial telephone exchange was opened in 1879, but when the company erected its necessary but disfiguring telephone poles two years later the merchants of the downtown area threatened to cut them down with axes. They were fighting for a lost cause. By the beginning of the new century the business section was a forest of wooden poles. In addition to those carrying the telephone lines, there were three private companies supplying electric power to industries, businesses and residences which also used the now ubiquitous creosoted two-storey sticks. Then there was the maze of cross-street wiring required by the London Street Railway which exchanged its horse-drawn cars for electric trolleys in 1895. The change these developments made in the appearance of the city was dramatic—and ugly. The poles and wires obscured the view and made even the most exciting events seem somehow mechanized.

The most stirring happening of the dying century was the departure of London troops for the South African War in 1899. As a garrison town London had many times seen uniformed men marching off to the defence of the Empire—in 1837, to put down the Mackenzie rebellion; in 1853, when the British garrison was emptied for service in the Crimea; in 1866 for the Fenian Raids; in 1870 for the Northwest Rebellion and again in 1885 for the Riel Rebellion. None of these occasions however had wakened the patriotic fervour of the average Londoner to the same extent as Canada's participation in Great Britain's most unpopular war. The empire fever was at its height following the emotional impact of Victoria's two jubilees. Then too, the American newspapers strongly disapproved of the war and anything the press of the United States condemns is bound to receive the equally strong approval of London's citizens.

Beginning on November 2, 1899, daily services of prayer "for the Army, in South Africa" were held in St. Paul's Cathedral. Attendance at first was heavy but as time went on interest diminished and the services were allowed to drop in May, 1900.

Queen Victoria died before the successful termination of the war. With her died an era. Its vestiges lingered on for decades particularly in provincial towns like London, but even the most stubborn Victorian knew in his secret heart that the world would never be the same again.

King Edward VII, that bon-vivant who as the nineteen-year-old Prince of Wales had captured the hearts of London's society belles on his visit to the city in 1860, was crowned on August 9, 1902. A special coronation service was held in St. Paul's Cathedral on the occasion. The new peal of bells presented through the generosity of Mr. Justice ˙R. M. Meredith rang out from the old bell tower to greet the new monarch's reign.

It was a time for the severing of old ties and the formation of new ones. On July 19, 1903, Dean Innes preached his last sermon. Less than two weeks later his funeral attracted one of the largest congregations in the history of the cathedral.

The saintly-looking dean with the bushy Dundrearies had been connected with the cathedral longer than any other man except Bishop Cronyn. A native of Weymouth, Devonshire, England, where he was born on January 21, 1826, he was a son of the parsonage, his father being the Reverend John Bontel Innes, a cousin of the Duke of Roxborough.

The younger Innes was educated at Mill-Hill Grammar School and Sandhurst Military College. He received his commission in the British Army in 1849 and was immediately sent to Canada where he served for twelve years with the Royal Canadian Rifles, a British regiment partially recruited in this country. He retired with the rank of captain in 1861 and continued the theological studies he had begun while still in uniform. He was made deacon in 1862 and priest the following year.

With the exception of one brief period as assistant at the Anglican cathedral in Quebec City the whole of Dr. Innes' ministry was served at St. Paul's Cathedral. The story has already been told of his work in connection with the establishment of Christ Church, London, the oldest of the parishes branching off from the cathedral. During his thirty-six years' association with St. Paul's as assistant curate, curate, rector and dean he played a key role in the founding of four other congregations, besides Christ Church. The congregation of Cronyn Memorial Church grew out of services in a small chapel at the corner of King and Adelaide streets held by Dean Innes. Similarly St. James' (Westminster) developed from Dr. Innes' ministry in a schoolhouse as did St. George's in West London. He also assisted in the foundation of the Church of St. John the Evangelist.

For the space of a generation the cathedral and its huge old rectory had been associated with the Innes name. The rectory had become in the truest sense the home of the Innes family. The dean loved the old building. Indeed it was said its later occupants or their domestics on more than one occasion saw what they reported to be the earthbound ghost of the dean making tours of inspection of his former domain. No one knows what happened to the gentle shade when the rectory was replaced in 1955 by a tall concrete-and-glass office building.

Bishop Baldwin did not long survive the dean, dying in October, 1904. His successor was the Reverend David Williams of Stratford who had been briefly curate at the cathedral in 1889/90. The dean's successor as rector of St. Paul's was the Reverend Alfred G. Dann, a canon of the Church of Ireland who had been assistant rector at St. Paul's since 1895. The Venerable Archdeacon Evans Davis, rector of St. James (Westminster) Church was named Dean of Huron.

The deaths of Bishop Baldwin and Dean Innes marked the end of a church era in London as definitely as the death of Queen Victoria signalled the end of a social epoch. Both were in a very real sense "shepherds of the flock." They were men of spiritual authority rather than of administrative genius. They were men of saintly bearing and saintly acts.

The growth of the church and the weight of administrative responsibilities made the Baldwin-Innes type obsolescent. Their like and their times will not return again in our generation and we are the poorer for it.

CHAPTER THIRTEEN

WAR AND PEACE

When the host goeth forth against thine enemies, then keep thee from every wicked thing.

Deuteronomy 23: 9

There is a curious parallel between the terms of office of the third, fourth and fifth rectors of St. Paul's and the reigns of the contemporary British monarchs. Dean Innes' term covered almost two-thirds of Queen Victoria's reign. His successor, Canon Dann, rector from 1903 to 1910, served a term roughly synchronizing with that of Edward VII and Dean L. N. Tucker (1911-1934) came very close to paralleling the reign of George V.

The problems faced by the rectors were, in minature, the problems faced by the kings. Dean Innes presided over the destinies of St. Paul's through the slow disintegration of the long Victorian peace. Canon Dann led his congregation through the gay and opulent but uneasy Edwardian era. Dean Tucker, with the gallantry and dignity belonging to an age already lost beyond recall, helped his faltering people through the shocks and losses of history's first global war, the insanity of the postwar boom and the shattering despair of global depression.

The changes that followed in the wake of these ruptures in the body international were inevitably reflected in the life and living of the people of London, but they came late and with great reluctance.

Physically, the city changed but little in the three decades following Dean Innes' death. The limits moved very slightly outward with the acquisition of suburbs to the south and east. Natural increase coupled with the backwash of the immigration policy of the Liberal administration of Sir Wilfrid Laurier boosted the population respectably but modestly. From 39,000 in 1900, it rose to 75,000 in 1935, the greatest periods of increase being between 1910 and 1915, (12,000) and between 1925 and 1930, (7,000).

The outward aspect of the city revealed its inward character to the observant eye. It was immutable, impenetrable and impervious to the scorn of "foreigners," which included anyone whose family origins were outside London. It was in short, in these decades, a typical Canadian small town which obstinately refused to grow up.

It was proud of its wide tree-shaded boulevards and its high percentage of home-ownership. It was proud of its arch-conservatism and insularity and complacently insolent in its pride. It turned a deaf ear to the gibes of outsiders who called it "the world's largest village" and "the place where all good farmers go to die." It acknowledged the existence of that part of the world which lay within the embrace of Lakes Huron, St. Clair and Erie but was politely sceptical about whatever lay outside.

The London of the period under review has been compared to Victoria, British Columbia, as an anachronistic survival of the era of Victorian imperialism. The comparison is not apt. In Victoria, the sun of empire has not yet set. London has never set its full seal of approval on either empire or republic. It respects both, but prefers to reserve judgment.

The use of the present tense in the above paragraph is intentional and deliberate. The habits of thought engendered by generations of stubborn conservatism still provide the bedrock for London's (and Victoria's) instinctive intellectual machinery. Although the climate is changing and the bedrock crumbling under the dynamic impact of the twentieth century, it is still possible for outsiders to be baffled by the complex and apparently irrational nature of the collective London character. A brilliant Presbyterian cleric once explained the inexplicable to a new Dean of Huron in these words:

Mister Dean, I have lived in London for twenty-two years and I can tell you that it is different from any other place on God's

green earth. Indeed I have been told on good authority that it
was a separate creation . . . And Mister Dean . . . after twenty-two
years here, I am inclined to agree!

Separate creation or not, the iron immutability of London's
character has perplexed many an observer, who has not taken
the trouble to look behind the external façade to discover the
true causes, which are simple enough. Here in London the
clash of American expansionism and British imperialism
which produced that new breed, the English-Canadian, is
most clearly exemplified. The native Londoner is merely a
super-Ontarian, honed by four generations of tradition to a
razor edge.

Tradition, nurtured by long years of comparative isolation
and insulation from the *sturm und drang* of the world outside, is a major factor in the city's character. For years
Londoners complained about the antiquated nature of the
Middlesex County courthouse and the Canadian National
Railway station. Occasionally federal or provincial authorities
have made the mistake of taking these complaints seriously.
In 1936 the old CNR station (designated "temporary" in
1854) was replaced, shocking the critics of the old structure
into a somewhat hurt silence. In 1964 the Middlesex County
grand jury condemned the courthouse as "inadequate" for
the one hundred and eleventh consecutive year. However, a
subsequent proposal for its demolition and replacement
brought cries of distress from a majority of the inhabitants.

The foregoing however, is only the reverse side of the
coin; the negative print which must be developed to establish
a true and recognizable portrait.

Thus, London's preoccupation with tradition is not a dead
and useless piece of community baggage. It expresses itself
in a true love of history, its own and those of other people,
as circulation figures at the London Public Library will attest.
There is little in this interest of the sterile aggrandizement of
one's own ancestors such as mark the activities of the
Daughters of the American Revolution or the United Empire
Loyalist Association. Its University of Western Ontario has

attracted some of the finest scholars of history in the nation. In no other city in Canada do items of historical interest consistently receive bigger or more frequent headlines in the local press.

Although London's arch-conservatism has resulted often in the conservation of outmoded attitudes to the point of petrefaction, it has also contributed to the preservation of fine cultural traditions. It has supported, for more than a century, an amateur theatre which has become the world's largest, and it has encouraged, for as long a period, a succession of musical enterprises which have made London famous throughout the continent.

Economically, London's conservatism (born in the cruel travail of the depression of 1857-1859) has protected the city from many of the blunders that brought many other Canadian cities to the point of bankruptcy in the 1930's. No other city in Canada enjoys more security in its municipal financing; the stability of its leading financial and mercantile establishments is well known everywhere.

Londoners' pride in their city's tree-shaded boulevards has developed over the years a love of open spaces which has preserved the city from overcrowding and resulted in an excellent network of parks and public recreational areas. It has also helped them to resist for ninety years the blandishments of speculators and "developers" anxious to turn London's downtown city park—Victoria Park—to commercial uses and transform its fourteen acres of grass and trees into a forest of concrete and glass boxes.

In sum, while London may not claim to be unique among the cities of the world, it has maintained what may rightly be considered an unusual blend of British and American attitudes, of nineteenth- and twentieth-century standards, of economic stability and cultural uncertainty. In short it is probably the most typically Canadian of all Canadian cities.

In the development of these distinctive features the congregation of St. Paul's has played a not inconsiderable role. Its influence, nakedly to be seen in the power structure of the community's early years, became more subtle but nonetheless powerful with the passage of time. The period under review

(which has been for a time sidetracked by more or less philo-
sophical considerations) saw that influence slowly undermined
by the cataclysmic changes convulsing the world outside.

It was Canon Dann's privilege to preside over the spiritual
destinies of the congregation during that brief and elegant
entr'acte between the Boer War and what we used to call the
"Great War." Canon Dann was by all acounts a scholarly man,
a product of that evangelical Irish church tradition that had
given St. Paul's its first rector. He effected no great changes
during his rectorship but left the physical fabric of the church
in better condition than he had found it and its moral fibre
strengthened against the shocks that would soon assail it.

One of his first duties as rector was to assist at the consecration and enthronement of the fourth Bishop of Huron. The
Venerable David Williams, rector of Stratford and Archdeacon of Perth, was elected by the Huron Synod on November 29, 1904, and enthroned in the cathedral church (where
he had once served as assistant) on Epiphany Day, 1905. The
group photograph taken on that occasion shows a collection
of ecclesiastical sideburns, moustaches and beards that comes
as something of a shock to a generation accustomed to bare-
faced clergy.

January, 1905, was a busy month for the cathedral. After
witnessing the consecration of its bishop the congregation
turned its attention to the celebration of an anniversary—its
seventieth, according to an excellent booklet compiled for the
occasion by Canon Dann. It should be remarked here that
until very recently there has been no unanimity as to the
ascription of a date for the establishment of this congregation.
A wide range of dates has been used for "anniversary" purposes, ranging from 1832 to 1846. As a formal congregation
of the Church of England in Canada, the proper date for
its establishment is probably August, 1829—when the Reverend E. J. Boswell arrived in London and founded the
London mission. The date for the formal opening and consecration of the first church is correctly September 14, 1834.

Canon Dann's little history of the church is the best and
most accurate of the many commemorative pieces published

over the years, even if the wording and spelling of the inscriptions on the memorial tablets in the church are not always correct.

A brief but interesting account is given of the cathedral choir which under the skilled direction of George B. Sippi had become one of the most highly-respected organizations of its kind in Western Ontario. Another member of the Sippi family (and who can help sympathizing with Mrs. Sippi?), Dr. Charles Sippi, one of the outstanding Canadian singers of the day was leading tenor of the choir from 1875 until his death in 1906.

There had been a gradual change from the stark, evangelical simplicity of the music of the cathedral's early years. Beginning in 1883 the choir wore surplices, originally the gift of Mrs. E. W. Hyman. By 1905 Canon Dann could report that the choir "for some years . . . has given a full cathedral service, as given in the cathedrals of the Old Country."

This is borne out by surviving church bulletins for Easter and Christmas services during this period, the versicles, canticles and Psalms all being sung. Most of the settings, the anthems included, were by Maunder.

Music, like true love, is seldom without its little crises. This is particularly true of church music. Few churches have managed to survive as long as St. Paul's without a record of disputes in and out of the choir loft. Whether this is due to the artistic temperament or to the intransigeance of rector and congregation is best left to the arbitration of a higher authority. Certainly it is impossible at this remove of time to judge of the differences that developed between the choir of St. Paul's and its rector and congregation early in the twentieth century when George B. Sippi resigned his post as organist and choir director.

Whatever the cause, the choir acted on its provocation in a most dramatic way. They declared a total strike. Their action made front-page headlines in the local press. In this emergency a committee of the congregation was formed headed by Mrs. E. B. Smith (later Mrs. Shannon). The committee called for volunteers from the congregation and as a consequence over seventy men and women turned up for rehearsal. They were equipped with makeshift surplices (some of them made out of sheets) and turned out for services the following Sunday. Due to the newspaper publicity the cathedral was crowded for the occasion. A great many of the volunteer choir members remained in that capacity, some for a period of years. The first soloist was Lady Beck, wife of the father of Ontario hydro-electric power.

Some years later a similar situation developed (in October, 1929) when the then organist and choirmaster, Harry Dickenson, resigned after a dispute with the rector, Dean Tucker. Although no strike ensued, the unfortunate argument left a core of discontent for some time.

In other ways too the cathedral was changing with the times. Just as in the 1850's it had been one of the first public buildings in London to be lit by gas so fifty years later it became one of the first to use electricity. London was a pioneer in the use of electrical power, thanks largely to the inspiration of one of its leading citizens, Sir Adam Beck, founder of the Ontario Hydro-Electric Power Commission.

In certain other respects the church resisted change. When *The London Free Press* introduced "The Yellow Kid", harbinger of a veritable flood of comic strips, all of London's churches unleashed an ecumenical torrent of abuse on the publishers, who meekly ditched the feature. It was with considerable trepidation, in view of this scarring experience, that *The Free Press* and its rival, *The London Advertiser*, began about 1904 to advocate the introduction of a Sunday street car service. The reaction from the churches—St. Paul's included —was immediate, vocal, loud and hysterical. The battle raged for ten years and ended with the victory of the common man who, having neither a carriage nor one of the new-fangled automobiles, otherwise had to walk to church. As finally inaugurated in 1914 the Sunday public transport service began (and still does) at 10 A.M.—useful enough for those attending 11 o'clock worship but of no value whatever to those bound for early communion.

Amid these alarums and excursions on the local scene the congregation of St. Paul's turned its attention to the neglected

fabric of the cathedral and its rectory. The extensive alterations of 1892-1894 had absorbed all available funds but had
not included necessary repairs, painting and roofing of the
exterior of the church and rectory. These needed improvements were effected in 1910 and saddled the church with a
new mortgage debt of some $14,000 which it required nearly
twenty years to liquidate.

Scarcely had the work been completed than the cathedral
was deprived of its rector. Canon Dann died in Bristol, England, on July 24, 1910. The day following he would have
marked the 39th anniversary of his ordination to the priesthood. He was succeeded as rector of St.Paul's by the Reverend
Canon L. Norman Tucker, still affectionately remembered by
many Londoners.

The new rector (created Dean of Huron in 1917) took on
his capable shoulders the load of debt left by his predecessor
and in the course of his twenty-three-year incumbency not
only discharged the mortgage but presided over the enlarge-
ment of Cronyn Hall and the fitting-out of the south transept
as a chapel (1924).

Less pleasant duties fell to the lot of the fifth rector of St.
Paul's. He preached in the cathedral on that hot and muggy
August Sunday when the lights went out in Europe and the
armies began to march. The cathedral's Book of Remembrance
tells the bitter story of the four years of hell that followed.
The congregation watched some of its finest young men march
away and watched some of them returning. Neither the
cathedral nor its people, its city or its world, would ever be
quite the same again.

The Preachers' Book of the period, recording the daily and
weekly services, contains surprisingly few references to the
vast conflict taking place in Europe. An occasional service of
intercession, a memorial service in November, 1915 for nurse
Edith Cavell (shot as a spy by the Germans)—are the only
evidences of the strain the congregation was sustaining. It
was not until the last month of the war that its meaning came
home to St. Paul's with stunning impact. The war-spawned
influenza epidemic of 1918-19 caused civilian casualty lists
that at times occupied two full pages (in small type) in the

local newspaper press. During the height of the epidemic—
the latter half of October, 1918—St. Paul's in common with
all London's churches, schools, theatres and other places of
public assembly, was completed closed up. This was the only
time in the history of St. Paul's that all weekday and Sunday
services were suspended.

The war-wrought change in London's way of life was
sudden and shocking. New words appeared in the vocabu-
lary overnight—"tank," "zeppelin," "rationing," "female franchise." The world was in upheaval, revolution was abroad,
and St. Paul's was not to remain unscathed. To the old
guard, the revolution that racked Russia in October, 1917, was
scarcely less astonishing than the action of Dean Tucker in
the preceding month when he welcomed the presence of
women for the first time at a cathedral vestry meeting. It
had long been recognized by clergy and laity alike that
women were a powerful force in the church but it seemed
faintly improper formally to acknowledge this fact. The test
of time has proved their inestimable worth in the official
councils of the church.

Revolutions in politics were followed by revolution in manners, style and customs. In the feverish decades following the
armistice of 1918 dresses got shorter, manners and morals
became freer and church attendance dwindled. Religious
scepticism, nurtured by popular misconceptions of the theories
of Charles Darwin, Karl Marx and Albert Einstein, claimed
ever more adherents among the disillusioned postwar generation and church populations gradually dropped to an all-time
low. It was to take the threat of universal annihilation by
thermonuclear weapons to bring them back.

It was Dean Tucker's unhappy responsibility to shepherd
his congregation through the most trying times in its history
—war, postwar hysteria and depression. Through it all he
moved with calm dignity and all-encompassing compassion
and understanding. When, on January 6, 1926, he celebrated
the fiftieth anniversary of his ordination, the church was
packed to do him honour. The service was preached by the
Bishop of Huron, shortly himself to be honoured by being

made archbishop and metropolitan of the ecclesiastical province of Ontario.

Many of the "elder statesmen" of the diocese and the Anglican Church today were affected in one way or another by the life and Christian service of Dean Tucker. For example in February, 1917, he took part at the ordination to the priesthood of the Reverend Clarence W. Foreman, now and for many years past rector of the Church of St. John the Evangelist in London and venerable archdeacon of the deanery of Middlesex East. Archdeacon Foreman served for some time as assistant to Dean Tucker as did also the Reverend Denny Bright, the Reverend (now Canon) E. Lightbourn and the Reverend M. Bernard Johnson. It was also during Dean Tucker's rectorship that the cathedral's veteran lay reader, Major A. G. N. Bradshaw began his long years of service.

According to the Preachers' Book, the 11 A.M. communion service of July 1, 1934, marked "the last time Dean Tucker was in church and the last sermon he preached." He died shortly after and the entire community mourned the passing of a truly Christian gentleman.

CHAPTER FOURTEEN

WAR AND PEACE

(continued)

Wisdom is better than weapons of war; but one sinner destroyeth much good.
—Ecclesiastes 9: 18

The Most Reverend David Williams, Archbishop of Huron and Metropolitan of Ontario, died on October 7, 1931. The synod elected the Right Reverend Dr. Charles Allen Seager, then bishop of the Diocese of Ontario, as fifth Bishop of Huron. Three years later the fifth bishop inducted the sixth rector of St. Paul's Cathedral, Charles Edward Jeakins, naming him at the same time Dean of Huron.

Dean Jeakins, a happy, out-going man, a native of York-shire, England, directed the work of the cathedral at a time when laughter was sorely needed. His short term began at the peak of the great depression (1934) and ended as the world was being plunged into the second global war in a generation. He was equal to his task. Unlike his predecessor who was deeply immersed in the work of the church to the exclusion of most outside activities, Dean Jeakins played an active role in community life, being especially involved in the work of the London Kiwanis Club. He had been a district governor of Kiwanis while living in Brantford, prior to his removal to London.

The five years of his rectorship were marked by many changes in the community. The population slowly rose to 76,000 and stuck there for four years. It was to take fifteen more years to reach the 100,000 mark, and then it stalled there for six years. Nevertheless the growth of the community between 1934 and 1960 was phenomenal. The population figures hide a development London has shared with all other North American cities.

143

By the mid-1930's the lemming-like flight to the suburbs had begun.

Whether from a desire to evade city taxes, an urge to "return to the land" or a compulsion to emulate the Jones's, hundreds of London families of the middle and higher income brackets, bought or built homes just outside the city limits. New neighbourhoods sprang up, the neighbourhoods became suburbs, the suburbs became communities and by the end of the fifth decade of the twentieth century almost as many Londoners lived outside the city limits as lived within them.

These changes were reflected in the life of the cathedral. Many former parishioners of St. Paul's transferred their allegiance to churches nearer their suburban retreats or lost contact altogether with their church. It was to be the task of the eighth rector of St. Paul's, the present bishop of Huron, to try to rectify this situation by taking the church to these voluntary exurbanites.

During Dean Jeakins' term the dimensions of this geographical change were only beginning to make themselves manifest. Man's effect on his natural environment showed itself in a much more dramatic fashion in the spring of 1937. In the late afternoon of April 26 the floodwaters of the Thames River, no longer restrained as they had once been by dense forest cover on the watershed, spilled over their banks and inundated 1,050 homes on the river flats in the western and southern portions of the city. Foresighted men had warned that this might happen, but few paid them any attention—until April 26, 1937.

Because of adequate warning only one life was lost, but thousands of people were made temporarily homeless and damage ran into the millions of dollars. Every public and private agency in the community turned to the job of rescue, comfort and rehabilitation. In this work the congregation of St. Paul's played no small part.

Despite depression and disaster the congregation made many improvements to the physical fabric of its buildings in Dean Jeakins' five years. In 1935 and 1936 a total of $6,200 was spent in repairs to the rectory. Gifts were made of a new carpet for the chancel and sanctuary, new choir stalls, chapter

stalls and prayer desks. Another donation made it possible to
have the tower bells recast, enlarged and retuned in England.
The rehabilitated bells were heard for the first time on Christmas Day, 1935. At the keyboard was Fred Kingsmill, who has
been ringing the bells of St. Paul's for nearly sixty years.
When Fred's concert was finished he pencilled a note of the
date and occasion on one of the walls of the bell-ringers' loft.
His inscription keeps company there with scores of other
notations covering a period of nearly a century. Some of the
graffiti are so old as to be nearly indecipherable. The names of
many of the bell-ringers have been all but forgotten, but none
of the generation of Londoners now living will ever be able
to hear or think about the bells of St. Paul's without thinking
of Fred Kingsmill, who helps to run his family's large department store as a sideline.

London had almost become used to the depression—to the
heavy drain on public taxes for relief measures, the pan-
handlers and the long lines of hopeless applicants at the employment agencies—when Adolf Hitler, the hysterical little
man with the funny moustache, plunged the world into war.

The "phoney war" of the winter of 1939-40 had passed, the
"impregnable" Maginot Line had been overwhelmed, the
panzer divisions had smashed the Low Countries into sub-
mission and France had fallen when Dean Jeakins died and
Bishop Seager announced the name of his successor. He was
the Reverend Canon Percival Nathaniel Harding, rector of
All Saints' Church, Windsor. Canon Harding, who was
named rector of St. Paul's and Dean of Huron in November,
1940, was a native of Lucan who served his entire ministry
in the Diocese of Huron and in four charges only: All Saints,
Windsor (1913-1917 and 1926-1940); St. Saviour's, Waterloo
(1917-1921); St. John's, St. Thomas (1921-1926) and St.
Paul's, London (1940-1944).

The appointment of Dean Harding by Bishop Seager
marks an interesting landmark in the history of the cathedral.
For the first time not only were both the bishop and the
dean of Huron Canadian natives, but they were both natives
of the diocese. The old days of dependence upon the Mother
Church for both men and money were gone.

Dean Harding, a humble dedicated man, made a deep impression on the spiritual life of St. Paul's. In his short rectorship of less than four years he left little or no mark on the physical structure of the church. Not for him the tasks of restoration, reconstruction or renovation. He worked within the hearts and souls of men. His memorial is the cathedral Servers' Guild which he organized and to which he gave many hours of devoted service.

The comment that appeared in *The Parish Messenger* on the occasion of the memorial service for Dean Harding on the first Sunday in Lent (February 27) 1944, adequately sums up his life and works:

Simplicity, kindness, humility and love characterized our beloved Dean's whole life. He will be remembered as following in that succession of consecrated parish priests, whose ministry has been at once the pride and glory of the Church of England. He loved God and served Him in his work for the poor, the needy, the lonely and the underprivileged no less than for those who from positions of great responsibility looked to him for guidance.
Each time the Te Deum is sung in this Cathedral, which he loved, we may include him in its prayer—
"Make them to be numbered with thy saints, in glory everlasting."

In that same Lenten season of 1944 high honour came to the Diocese of Huron and to St. Paul's when Bishop Seager was enthroned in his cathedral church as archbishop and metropolitan of Ontario—the second time the distinction had come to the diocese.

One of the new archbishop's first jobs was to appoint a successor to Dean Harding. His choice fell upon the Reverend George Nasmith Luxton who was accordingly installed as rector of St. Paul's and Dean of Huron in a service at the cathedral on September 27, 1944.

Dean Luxton faced a monumental task of physical reconstruction. While much money had been laid out over the years on the cathedral's buildings, most of it had been spent on emergency repairs, a bit at a time. No major renovation had been undertaken since the turn of the century. Walls, roof, ceiling and tower all needed attention, desperately.

The new dean was equal to the problem. This was a young, energetic man who came to the post at the peak of his powers. Under his dynamic leadership the congregation embarked on a series of renewals and replacements. To dramatize the need for renovation of one of the city's most outstanding historic landmarks, special attention was paid to the cathedral's various centenaries. In December, 1944, the one hundredth anniversary of the beginning of work on the present building was celebrated and again in December, 1946, the centenary of its completion. If some slight injury was done thereby to the strict chronology of the church, it was in a good cause. The actual dates in both cases occur in the Lenten season when celebration, in the secular sense. is out of place.

In addition to extensive repairs to the church, the chancel and sanctuary were beautified by the erection of eleven symbolic shields set into the ceiling. These were painted by the firm of A. W. R. McDougall, of Toronto, and have been much admired. The ancient symbols include the dove, representing the Holy Ghost; the man, St. Matthew; the lion of St. Mark, the ox of St. Luke and the eagle of St. John.

Scarcely had the work of restoration been completed when the diocese was saddened by the death of Archbishop Seager on September 9, 1948. At the ensuing meeting of synod Dean Luxton was elected sixth Bishop of Huron. He was consecrated and enthroned in St. Paul's on November 30.

On December 6 Bishop Luxton announced the appointment of the Reverend Canon Richard Charles Brown, a graduate of Montreal Diocesan Theological College, then rector of All Saints, Windsor, as rector and dean, effective January 1, 1949.

Dean Brown's rectorship of a little more than twelve years witnessed more changes in the community and in the life of the cathedral than any similar period since the founding of the congregation in 1829. When he took up his post London was a city of 92,000 persons living within a 10.9-square mile area; when he resigned the rectorship in April, 1961, the city's population had risen to 165,000 and its boundaries enclosed an urban sprawl of 63.37 square miles—in physical area the largest city in Ontario with the sole exception of Toronto.

The economic expansion of the 1950's beggared the great land boom of a century before but it was fortunately built on a much more solid foundation. War-spawned industries stayed on when the war was over and others came to join them. London suddenly found itself, to its great surprise, counted among the industrial cities of the province. The town where "good farmers go to die" had become an important business centre and was slated to become even more important. London had always occupied a phenomenally high position among the cities of Canada with respect to income tax returns, but very low with respect to bank clearing figures. Now clearing house figures rose steadily up the scale. London's "frozen capital" was on the move. A new crop of millionaires appeared on the scene and some of them were quite as colourful as the swash-buckling merchant princes of the city's village days.

Landmarks untouched by a century of change began to tumble before the march of progress. In the year of London's centennial as an incorporated city—1955—an Anglican landmark bowed to the bulldozers. The rectory of St. Paul's, which despite many alterations and renovations had become obsolete and inadequate, made way for a concrete, steel and green glass seven-story office building.

In the years since the official establishment of the London parish in 1836, much of the church's original property had been sold in an effort to meet the ever-mounting load of debt. The temptation to do so was great as the growth of the community increased the value of the cathedral's midtown holdings. By 1955 the original square-block tract of 1836 had been reduced by more than seventy-five per cent.

There had been a gradual hardening of the attitude opposing further sales of church land inaugurated, it is said, by Dean Tucker. Consequently, when the proprietors of "200 Queens Limited" approached the cathedral board of management it was with a proposal to lease the rectory land for a period of ninety-nine years. This period was a mere moment in time compared with the 999-year rental arrangement under which the cathedral in its turn held its land from the synod. A general meeting of the congregation unanimously—on behalf of itself, its sons and grandsons—approved the deal and the rectory was pulled down in August of 1955. A feature of the transaction which appealed to the people of St. Paul's was that the rentals over the period of the lease amounting in total to close to a million dollars would eventually permit the church to repurchase much of its "lost" property.

The following year a development of more spiritual significance was begun at the cathedral. An article by Kae McColl, published in *Weekend Magazine* in its issue of February 7, 1959, briefly and succinctly describes the pattern of the St. Paul's weekday Lenten services:

Ten minutes before noon on every weekday during Lent, the bells of St. Paul's Cathedral ring out over downtown London. As the last chime dies away, between 500 and 600 worshippers—business and professional men, stenographers, clerks, students, shoppers and housewives—hurry into the church for a 25-minute service designed to fit easily into their lunch hour.
After listening to an outstanding Canadian or American minister, they can be in and out of a cafeteria in the adjoining church hall for a cost-price lunch in a further twelve minutes.

The services which began in the Lenten season of 1956 have been continued since with no change and have been widely copied by churches in other Canadian cities. No emphasis has been placed on denomination, and guest speakers have run the gamut of the Christian faiths. For the last two years the presence of a Roman Catholic priest in St. Paul's pulpit has drawn "full houses."

In 1957 the Diocese of Huron marked the centenary of its founding with appropriate services and special events. Among the latter was a one-hour television documentary (sponsored by the diocesan radio and television committee) which detailed some of the highlights of the previous hundred years. An incident which occurred during the preparation of one of the filmed sequences used in the production deserves telling.

The script called for an opening sequence on film in which the camera from a position a half block away from the cathedral's front entrance slowly moved towards the great front doors (the correct technical description is "dollied in"), through the narthex and up the centre aisle to the chancel steps, concluding with a final "zoom close-up" of the high altar.

A number of difficulties were faced by the producers in filming this apparently simple sequence. The exterior portion was eventually put on film by mounting the camera on the nose of a small sports car with the camera-man sitting on the bonnet. A small ramp was placed over the curb to prevent any joggling of the camera as it moved up over the curb, across the public sidewalk, through the stone gate-posts at the entrance to the cathedral, and up the cathedral sidewalk to the front doors.

With the co-operation of a member of London's constabulary who held up traffic on Richmond Street for the passage of the converted MGA (piloted with skill and cunning by the author's wife—the wrong way on a one-way street, by courtesy of the police department), the first objective was attained on the first—or it may have been the second—crack.

Then came the interior sequence. This too, should have been a relatively simple operation but was not, owing to the condition of the cathedral's ancient flooring. After the passage of thousands of feet over a period of one hundred and eleven years, the floor was rippled like the varves on a Swedish lake. This problem was finally overcome by lashing the camera to the handlebars of a bicycle, the tires of which had been made soft by letting out some air.

As the improvised camera dolly moved slowly up the centre aisle, its bicyclist-cameraman intent on his job, Dean Brown appeared at the transept entrance to Cronyn Hall and stood transfixed. Through some oversight no one had thought to warn him of the peculiar proceedings. The expression on his face as he watched the mounted invasion of St. Paul's Cathedral was unforgettable.

He has never since made reference to the incident. I am quite sure he considered it all part of a bad dream.

After a rectorship of a dozen years marked by many advances in the work of the church and restoration and beautification of the cathedral, Dean Brown was forced to resign his post in the spring of 1961 by reason of ill health. Bishop Luxton appointed him to the parish of St. Mary's, Walkerville, Ontario.

One of the last actions taken by the congregation of St. Paul's under Dean Brown's leadership concerned the role of the cathedral in its downtown parish. The people of St. Paul's had gradually become aware that they had lost contact with the population of that "inner city" which constituted their parish. They no longer knew the people who lived in the rabbit warrens at the city's core. Above and below the glass fronts that lined the streets of the business district, in decayed and sub-divided former mansions on the fringes of the business district hundreds of people lived who "knew not God" and most certainly knew not the interior of St. Paul's Cathedral.

The motion passed by the congregational meeting of October, 1960, was broad in its intent, even if as yet undefined as to plan. It read:

That we espouse the church's mission in the world by applying ourselves to the needs, the care and the evangelizing of the nominal Anglicans, the lapsed and the unchurched in our own parish area.

This resolution was to provide the spark for the latest and one of the most dramatic developments in the history of the inter-relationship of St. Paul's Cathedral and its community.

CHAPTER FIFTEEN

CHARITY

Thou tellest my wanderings: put thou my tears into thy bottle: are they not in thy book?

Psalm 56: 8

London had always known the poor—its own and the friendless drifters from other communities.

Each of its four generations had passed through communal disaster when the winds of calamity shrieked down many a chimney, turning modest success into abject poverty.

Each of its four generations had harboured, reluctantly, the armies of poor, friendless strangers who plod painfully into oblivion whenever economic collapse becomes national, rather than local or regional in character.

To protect itself from the importunities of the afflicted each of the city's four generations built up organizations of constantly increasing complexity to look to the poor and stricken on its behalf.

By 1896 the number of these organizations had proliferated to such an extent as to make necessary the establishment of Canada's first community welfare council—the Charity Organization Society of London, Ontario. The expressed purpose of the society was to co-ordinate the work of its fifty-odd member organizations so as to prevent overlapping and duplication of effort.

The first half of the twentieth century brought an even greater proliferation of private societies aimed at the elimination of specific ills among the citizenry. The crushing effects of the great depression of the thirties brought public monies into the field on a large scale—not freely and spontaneously offered, but under the pressure of vocal and dedicated social reformers whose political position was, necessarily, to the left of centre.

Since the mass of the Canadian people was also left of centre economically, there was little determined opposition to such use of the taxation dollar on the three levels of government—municipal, provincial and federal.

By the close of World War Two, in the glow of wartime prosperity and postwar expansion, the poor seemed to have disappeared. Certainly in London they were no longer to be seen by those who were givers and not recipients of charity. This attitude was promptly reflected in decreased donations to the annual community welfare fund, which found itself fallen on evil days.

But the poor had not departed. It was all illusion—like the art of the stage magician who directs the attention of his audience elsewhere while his hands cheat. It was not the poor who had left London but their audience.

In their headlong flight to suburbia, beginning before World War Two, the more affluent Londoners left behind in the heartland of the city a vacuum. This was speedily filled by the poor. Throughout the core of the city, one-time residences were divided and divided again into smaller and smaller units and rented at ever-increasing profits to the socially defeated. In the business section upper floors, above the glass-encased fronts of the luxury emporia, were turned into beaverboard-partitioned rabbit warrens where the unskilled, untrained and unusable could breed with their common-law wives still more problems for their friends in the suburbs.

Unfortunately suburbia does not know them. How can it be otherwise? The suburbanite's day is governed by rigid patterns. In the morning he fights his way to the office through a tangle of traffic and at night he fights his way back again, his mind divided between the imminent danger of collision and the frustrations of the day. His wife, shopping in the neighbourhood shopping plaza by day and the community culture bins by night, has likewise divorced herself from the realities of communal poverty. Even where their community "image" makes membership on the board of a social agency obligatory they are safely and antiseptically removed from the direct contact with stark poverty.

What has happened in London has happened in every city on the continent. The poor have gone underground. They have hidden themselves in the most obvious and hence least-suspected hiding place—the inner city.

Social workers, public health nurses and the clergy of the midtown churches know them. They form the great bulk of the clientele of the social agencies. Their numbers steadily increase as a mechanized civilization demands ever higher skills to run its machines. Those who by reason of low mentality or economic bars to educational opportunities are left behind in the race, gravitate inevitably to the secondary accommodations offered by the inner city where landlords do not care what happens to them so long as the rent is collected. There are no taboos in the core area as to race, colour, creed, legitimacy or number of children. Conformity may reign in the suburbs, but here all that matters is the next meal.

It was in response to the spiritual and material needs of these social outcasts that the congregation of St. Paul's Cathedral planted the seeds of its Core Area Project in the fall of 1960. The resignation of Dean Brown a few months later left the proposal in a still unformed stage. Fortunately the dean's successor was equal to the challenge.

On Sunday, May 27, 1961, Bishop Luxton announced from the pulpit of the cathedral his choice for the vacant rectorship. He was the Reverend Kenneth Bernard Keefe, incumbent of St. Mathias' Church, Westmount, Quebec.

The tenth rector of St. Paul's who became also tenth Dean of Huron, is a native of British Columbia and a graduate of the Anglican Theological College, Vancouver. He was ordered deacon in 1940 while serving as curate of St. Saviour's Church in that city. The following year, priested, he transferred to Montreal where he was assistant priest at the Church of the Ascension until joining the Canadian Army as a chaplain in 1943. After demobilization in 1946 he served at Christ Church Cathedral, Montreal, and in the parishes of Grace Church, Sutton, Quebec; St. Michael's Church, Sillery, Quebec, and St. Mathias', Westmount.

As a director of Montreal's Family Service Centre—a marital counselling agency—Dean Keefe had had experience in the community welfare field. He consequently had a more than passing interest in his new congregation's plan to involve itself in the life of the inner city which is its true parish.

Something over a year passed however, before the new rector could turn his energies towards this aspect of the parish's work. Then, in the winter of 1962/63, while the thoughts of the whole Anglican Communion were directed to the impending World Anglican Congress (held in Toronto in August, 1963) Dean Keefe organized a series of Sunday night meetings to discuss the needs of the core area. Specially-qualified people—particularly workers in the social welfare field—drawn from the community at large were invited to talk about areas of need within the community "at all age levels, particularly among those who live within our immediate downtown community but have no affiliation with any church."

As a result of these meetings a broad spectrum of human needs was revealed without, however, any clear picture emerging of what any individual church could do toward alleviating the misery that was known to exist.

This was the situation in the spring of 1963. There was a clear call to action, not at all incompatible with the missionary fervor inevitably associated with the forthcoming world congress of the church. The Anglican Church of Canada has always been aware that there are mission fields at home as well as abroad.

At this point the objective viewpoint of the writer of history must be exchanged for the subjectivity of one who writes of his own role in current events.

It had been acknowledged that, successfully to enter the new field, it would be necessary to have someone with experience in social service to direct the activities of the congregation. I came "on the market" in May, 1963, following ordination to the diaconate by Bishop Luxton direct from ten years as public relations director and assistant executive director of London's United Community Services.

Dean Keefe applied his not inconsiderable powers of persuasion first to the bishop and then to me. In consequence I found myself in September, 1963, assuming the task of helping the congregation of St. Paul's Cathedral to realize its goal.

The church's downtown mission work was given a sober title—the "Core Area Project"—indicative of the as-yet unspecified nature of the task. It was realized from the first that haste must be made slowly if CAP was to make any useful and permanent contribution to the social and spiritual health of the community. At the same time the enthusiasm of the congregation for its new task had to be maintained and the secular services of the community had to be assured that the church was not invading their field or attempting to usurp their functions.

To achieve the first and most important goal, the congregation had to be involved in the project. To achieve the second, the social agencies had to be consulted. To a limited extent, both have been achieved, within the first year's operation. Some sixty volunteers have become involved in the work of the project and much co-operative work has been done with the city's secular agencies. Neither achievement has matched, in degree, the congregation's full expectations, but a good beginning has been made.

A formal organization has been created with a guiding committee composed of community leaders in the social welfare field, most of them members of the congregation. This committee has sought and obtained membership in the city's community welfare council—The United Community Services. There are a number of active sub-committees—a management committee primarily responsible for policy-making, a clothing committee which operates a clothing depot from which, once a week, the needy may draw their requirements free of charge, a visiting committee which conducts a followup on the project's clients and four study committees which are currently examining the community's needs and resources in specified areas.

The four areas being studied represent the needs most nakedly revealed in the first year's operation. In that year more than two thousand interviews were granted to more than five hundred persons, most of them residents of the core area. The most common problems presented were alcoholism, economic deprivation, delinquency, both adult and juvenile, and the complex problems of the Indian resident.

These bald figures and equally bald statements conceal a seething maelstrom of human misery concentrated in an almost intolerable degree in the heart area of the city. Misery is the only common denominator. Each individual presenting his tattered credentials—an unemployment insurance certificate, his discharge papers from the army, a non-committal letter from a government department—wants only to be considered a person, in an impersonal civilization.

They come asking for material help—a meal order on a local restaurant, clothing, help with groceries, $25 or $50 or $100 to set them up in a business promising fantastic returns —but beneath it all is the desperate call for help of the lost, the defeated, the insecure. They seldom reveal themselves in the first interview but sooner or later comes the call, spoken or merely implied—"Is there a God?" "Show me how to find God" or "Help me to find myself!"

It is comparatively easy for the socially and financially secure to maintain a formal and ritually-correct relationship with their God while retaining their practical interest in the state of the market or the progress of the Mars-bound rocket, but for the poor and derelict his reality is present and urgent. The rich may defer consideration of the meaning of God until death presents itself; the poor live with death each day.

There has been no sudden and overwhelming influx of new converts as the result of CAP's first year of operation. A total of seven or eight people have been introduced into the full life of the church, another half dozen have been rehabilitated to some degree, socially and morally. But persons *are* being seen at cathedral services who a few years ago would not have come and who might not have been welcomed if they had come.

Perhaps this is the greatest miracle of the Core Area Project —the enthusiastic willingness of the congregation to accept and support, with both time and money, a work which offers little tangible achievement and presents with each problem solved, two more that are apparently insoluble.

The future of CAP depends squarely on an ever-increasing involvement of the congregation. It has been fairly pointed out that the work of the Core Area Project is merely that of any parish priest within his parish family. The difference is in the numbers of persons with problems and the use of the laity in dealing with those problems. CAP is simply an attempt to give real, practical meaning to the expression so commonly bandied about in The Christian Church these days—"the ministry of the laity."

It is not to be thought that while dealing with mission work on its own doorstep the congregation of St. Paul's has been unaware of its commitments in the world outside. St. Paul's and the diocese of which it is the see church were deeply involved in the World Anglican Congress of 1963. Huron College in London—the theological college established by the first bishop of Huron—was the site of the pre-Congress meetings where one of the most dramatic documents in the history of the Christian church was drawn up. This document—Mutual Responsibility and Interdependence in the Body of Christ—is a blueprint for a new and revitalized Anglican Communion.

St. Paul's is playing an active role in the realization of the goals adopted by the Toronto Congress. It has contributed heavily to the extension of the church in Africa and its rector was chairman of a committee of Anglican and United Church representatives which drew up in the fall of 1964 a proposal for the union of the two churches.

From time to time some philosopher speaking from an ivy-covered ivory tower on a university campus speaks in pontifical tones of the twentieth century as the "first post-Christian century."

These people really should go to church more often.

Preferably they should go to St. Paul's Anglican Cathedral in London, Ontario.

APPENDICES

APPENDIX A

THE BISHOPS OF HURON

The Right Reverend Benjamin Cronyn   1857-1871
For an excellent biography of the first Bishop of Huron, see *Benjamin Cronyn* by the late Dr. A. H. Crowfoot, published by the Diocese of Huron, 1957.

The Right Reverend Isaac Hellmuth   1871-1883
For a biography of Bishop Hellmuth, see *This Dreamer* by Dr. A. H. Crowfoot (Copp Clark: 1963)

The Right Reverend Maurice Scollard Baldwin   1883-1904

The Most Reverend David Williams   1905-1931
Third Metropolitan of the ecclesiastical province of Ontario and Archbishop of Huron, 1926-1931.

The Most Reverend Charles Allen Seager   1932-1948
Fourth Bishop of the Diocese of Ontario, 1926-1932; seventh Metropolitan of the ecclesiastical province of Ontario and Archbishop of Huron, 1943-1948.

The Right Reverend George Nasmith Luxton   1948-........

**The Right Reverend William Thomas Thompson Hallam
    1949-1956**
Fifth Bishop of Saskatchewan, 1931; first Bishop of Saskatoon, 1932-1949; assistant Bishop of Huron, 1949-1956.

The Right Reverend William Alfred Townshend   1955-........
Suffragan Bishop of Huron.

**The Right Reverend Harold Frederick Gaviller Appleyard
    1961-........**
Suffragan Bishop of Huron with the title Bishop of Georgian Bay.

159

APPENDIX B
THE DEANS OF HURON

The Very Reverend Isaac Hellmuth   1866-1871

The Very Reverend Michael Boomer   1871-1888

The Very Reverend George Mignon Innes   1888-1903

The Very Reverend Evans Davis   1903-1918

The Very Reverend Louis Norman Tucker   1919-1934

The Very Reverend Charles Edward Jeakins   1934-1940

The Very Reverend Percival Nathaniel Harding   1940-1944

The Very Reverend George Nasmith Luxton   1944-1948

The Very Reverend Richard Charles Brown   1949-1961

The Very Reverend Kenneth Bernard Keefe   1961-........

APPENDIX C
THE RECTORS OF ST. PAUL'S

The Reverend Benjamin Cronyn   1832-1866

The Very Reverend Isaac Hellmuth   1866-1871

The Very Reverend George Mignon Innes   1871-1903

The Reverend Canon Alfred George Dann   1903-1910

The Very Reverend Louis Norman Tucker   1911-1934

The Very Reverend Charles Edward Jeakins   1935-1939

The Very Reverend Percival Nathaniel Harding   1940-1944

The Very Reverend George Nasmith Luxton   1944-1948

The Very Reverend Richard Charles Brown   1949-1961

The Very Reverend Kenneth Bernard Keefe   1961-........

APPENDIX D

THE CHURCHWARDENS

Records for the early years of the congregation of St. Paul's are scanty; consequently no accurate list of churchwardens is available until 1843. From the surviving data, however, the names of the most active members of the vestry from 1829 to 1842 can be ascertained. Many of the men whose names follow probably served as wardens during this period.

Lawrence Lawrason, John Kent, George Kennedy, John Baptiste Askin, Captain Richard Browne, J. Parkinson, Dr. Hiram Davis Lee, William Haskett, John Hawkins, Edward Allen Talbot, John Harris.

One record for 1832 lists Lawrence Lawrason as rector's warden and Edward Allen Talbot as people's warden. In the following year, Captain Richard Browne signs himself as "acting churchwarden." From other records it appears that Lawrence Lawrason was rector's warden in 1839, 1840, 1841.

The list from 1843 to the present follows. In the traditional order the name of the rector's warden is followed by that of people's warden. Consecutive terms of office, as those of Lawrence Lawrason and William Warren Street are grouped inclusively by date.

1843	Lawrence Lawrason	John Harris
1844-1846	Lawrence Lawrason	William Warren Street
1847-1848	Charles Monsarrat	William Warren Street
1849-1857	Lawrence Lawrason	William Warren Street
1858-1860	Lawrence Lawrason	Samuel Peters
1861-1862	Lawrence Lawrason	Charles Hunt
1863	A. Greer	W. Watson
1864	Charles Hunt	W. Watson (rep. by) Wm. Elliott
1865	Charles Hunt	William Elliott
1866-1869	J. B. Strathy	Richard Bayly
1870-1874	J. B. Strathy	James Hamilton
1875-1876	Henry Dawson Long	James Hamilton
1877	John B. Laing	James Hamilton
1878	John Labatt	Henry Dawson Long
1879-1880	Henry Dawson Long	Richard Bayly
1881	Richard Bayly	John Labatt
1882-1883	John Labatt	Richard Bayly
1884-1887	William J. Reid	T. Herbert Marsh
1888	George Laing	John S. Pearce
1889-1899	W. J. Reid	John S. Pearce
1900-1901	W. J. Reid	W. T. Strong

1902-1903	J. Mattinson	W. T. Strong
1904	H. E. Gates	F. W. Farncombe
1905-1906	C. B. Hunt	J. Mattinson
1907-1912	Dr. W. H. Moorehouse	E. Paull
1913-1917	Dr. W. H. Moorehouse	J. Harley Brown
1918-1919	Dr. W. H. Moorehouse	J. M. Slater
1920	Dr. W. H. Moorehouse	C. W. Nicholls
1921	J. M. Slater	Dr. A. J. Grant
1922	Dr. A. J. Grant	J. S. McConkey
1923	J. S. McConkey	Lt.-Col. J. I. Carling
1924	Lt.-Col. J. I. Carling	Dr. J. G. Hunt
1925	Dr. J. G. Hunt	C. W. Nicholls
1926	C. W. Nicholls	J. McClary Moore
1927	J. McClary Moore	Col. W. J. Brown
1928	Col. W. J. Brown	Ernest B. Smith
1929	Ernest B. Smith	E. W. B. Eardley
1930	E. W. B. Eardley	Col. W. J. Brown
1931	Col. W. J. Brown	J. H. Duplan
1932-1933	Dr. J. G. Hunt	J. H. Duplan
1934-1935	J. H. Duplan	J. D. Isaacs
1936-1937	C. W. Nicholls	W. J. Ashplant
1938	W. J. Ashplant	R. H. Beattie
1939	R. H. Beattie	J. H. Duplan
1940-1943	J. H. Duplan	J. D. Hunt
1944-1945	J. H. Duplan	C. H. Mathewson
1946	R. H. Beattie	J. W. Carson
1947	T. C. Margrett	J. W. Carson
1948	T. C. Margrett	J. D. Harrison
1949	T. K. Stiles	J. D. Harrison
1950	T. K. Stiles	E. M. Kennedy
1951	R. W. Mitchell	E. M. Kennedy
1952	R. W. Mitchell	J. H. Moore
1953	J. A. Cairncross	J. H. Moore
1954	J. A. Cairncross	K. Moore
1955	J. A. Cairncross	K. Moore
1956	H. K. Boughner	W. A. Paull
1957	Dr. G. E. Hall	W. A. Paull
1958	Dr. G. E. Hall	J. B. Cronyn
1959	N. G. Burdick	J. B. Cronyn
1960	N. G. Burdick	Dr. D. G. Wilson
1961	K. Moore	Dr. D. G. Wilson
1962	J. W. Stiles	A. R. White
1963	J. W. Stiles	A. E. Clendinning
1964	A. E. Clendinning	Dr. D. W. B. Johnston
1965	Dr. D. W. B. Johnston	Dr. A. J. Harris
1966	Dr. A. J. Harris	D. E. McKillop

APPENDIX E

THE MEMORIALS

The whole physical fabric of St. Paul's Cathedral is of course a memorial to successive generations of London Anglicans. On the grounds and within the church there are individual memorials of special interest.

On the grounds—part of the original crown grant to the church —are to be found a number of grave markers dating back to the time when the churchyard was used as the town cemetery. Possibly the most interesting is the stone commemorating Lawrence Lawrason, Senior (1760-1830), a United Empire Loyalist whose son was for many years a churchwarden and outstanding benefactor of the church. Other stones mark the burying places of British Army officers and their families.

At the base of the pinnacles that cap the great tower of the cathedral can be seen stone shields bearing the date 1845—the year of the erection of the present church.

The walls of the tower are immensely thick, having been designed for a peal of six bells. The original bells were made in England and shipped across the Atlantic in a sailing vessel called *The British Empire*. They were drawn from Port Stanley to London by teams of oxen in 1850. In 1935, through the generosity of Mr. Justice R. M. Meredith, five of these bells were re-cast and with some additional metal make up the present peal of eleven bells. The remaining bell of the original peal now hangs in the tower of Cronyn Hall and is used to summon the congregation to the week-day offices.

In the narthex are several memorials of the cathedral's early years. On the south side is a reminder of the Crimean War. A large and very ornate slab set into the wall is a monument to the memory of Lieutenant-Colonel Chester and the officers and men of Her Majesty's 23rd Regiment of Royal Welch Fusiliers who fell at the battle of Alma. Other monuments lining the walls of the narthex recall the military "occupation" of London. A stone from Canterbury Cathedral and a piece of marble from St. Paul's Cathedral, London, England, are set into the wall on the left and right of the doors leading to the nave.

As one enters the nave the first object that meets the eye is a beautiful baptismal font of Carrara marble which commemorates the service to the church of the Very Reverend G. M. Innes, third rector of the church.

Four picture windows on the north and south sides of the nave are from the Tiffany studios in New York City and commemorate members of the Meredith family, long connected with the life of the cathedral.

The great windows in the transepts are thirty-two feet high. Each contains six hundred square feet of glass. The window frames alone weigh over five tons.

On the walls of the north transept are memorial tablets to early members of the congregation of St. Paul's, including Thomas Cronyn, eldest son of the first Bishop of Huron.

The great Book of Remembrance, prepared in 1951 by the late Lieutenant-Colonel Francis B. Ware, D.S.O., and the cathedral organ—rebuilt by Cassavant Frères, of St. Hyacinthe, Quebec, in 1955—form the cathedral congregation's tribute to those who served in the two world wars.

Of the many memorials to be seen in the chancel the dean's stall, commemorating the Very Reverend Michael Boomer, second Dean of Huron, the bishop's throne (a memorial to Bishop Cronyn) and the series of symbols painted on the chancel roof during the incumbency of the Very Reverend George N. Luxton, are of special interest.

Flags of the three services hang in the cathedral. The colours of six local regiments have been laid up here and hang in the chancel.

The five windows in the sanctuary commemorate prominent Londoners who were members of the congregation of St. Paul's. They were: Lawrence Lawrason, Junior, for many years police magistrate and a churchwarden of St. Paul's; the Reverend Benjamin Bayly who for forty years had charge of secondary schools in London, first as principal of the London Grammar School then as principal of the London Collegiate Institute; Nathaniel and Sarah Reid, early settlers of the town; Ellis Walton Hyman who established a tannery in London in 1835 which is still in operation; the Honourable George Jervis Goodhue, the city's first general merchant and first millionaire, and Dr. Walter Hoare Moorhouse, one of the founders of the medical school of the University of Western Ontario.

The alms bason in the sanctuary is one of two memorials in the church marking the tragic sinking of the river steamer *Victoria* in the Thames River on May 24, 1881, with the loss of more than two hundred lives. The bason was presented by the family of Marion Grace Barker in thanksgiving for her rescue. One of the windows on the north side of the nave is in memory of John Walsingham Cooke Meredith, one of the victims of the disaster.

Cast of "Cronyn"

to dear Sally
with all good
wishes - Marden

Best Wishes!
Diane Swallowell

Lynn Young.

Luck from
Sid Leech.

Lee Wilson

Sally with love
Hart K.

a brilliant idea
Why bother?
Best wishes.

Peter Matthews

Greg Barrett

Joe Benedoe

Michael A. Favell
the "adventurous boy"

Mark Pur...
from The Drunken Pig

Remember duty
old Carmichael!

Pat Barber.